DEVOTIONS

DEVOTIONS

Poems by Timothy Murphy

Preface by Dana Gioia

NDSU NORTH DAKOTA STATE UNIVERSITY PRESS

NDSU NORTH DAKOTA STATE UNIVERSITY PRESS

Dept. 2360, P.O. Box 6050, Fargo, ND 58108-6050
www.ndsu.edu/ahss/ndirs

DEVOTIONS
Poems by Timothy Murphy
Preface by Dana Gioia

First Edition

Cover image: "Man of Sorrows," woodcut by Charles Beck
Cover and interior design by Deb Tanner

International Standard Book Number: 978-0-911042-91-7
Library of Congress Control Number: 2016939853

Printed in the United States of America

Publisher's Cataloging-in-Publication
(Provided by Quality Books, Inc.)

Murphy, Timothy, 1951- author.
[Poems. Selections]
Devotions : poems / by Timothy Murphy ; preface by Dana Gioia.
pages cm
Includes index.
LCCN 2016939853
ISBN 9780911042917

1. Meditations. 2. Devotional poetry, American. 3. Spiritual life--Christianity. 4. Poetry. 5. Meditations. I. Title.

BV4832.3.M865 2017 242
QBI16-900078

∞ This paper meets the requirements of ANSI/NISO Z39.48-1992 (Permanence of Paper).

The Lord God has given me the tongue of the learned, that I may know when a wearied one needs it. He rouses me morning by morning, he wakens my ear to hear like the learned.

Isaiah 50:4

On a Theme from Job

No, not goodbye. We'll meet again as kin.
Long may I live to tread the paths you trod,
yet after worms corrupt my freckled skin
I know that in our flesh we shall see God.

Adieu

You left our mortal ranks,
me to my memories,
and only on my knees
does grief give way to thanks.

Contents

II. From Camp Wilderness to Prairie St. John's Hospital

III. Whoso List to Hunt

IV. In David's Line

V. Coda

Preface

Until quite recently a substantial amount of English-language poetry was Christian verse. This tradition stretched over a millennium from the earliest surviving Anglo-Saxon poems, such as *The Dream of the Rood*, to the works of modern masters such as T. S. Eliot and W. H. Auden. The English-speaking world was conceived, even by non-believers, as part of Christendom, and a religious worldview was everywhere evident in its literature, even when the subjects were not overtly spiritual. As Donald Davie observed in the "Introduction" to his *Oxford Book of Christian Verse*, "most of those Christians did not suppose that their Christianity stopped when they came out through the church-door." Religion provided the moral and symbolic framework for poetry on all subjects. Much of the writing, however, was specifically religious. It would be impossible to trace the history of poetry in English without recognizing the centrality of spiritually engaged Christians—a line that included Edmund Spenser, George Herbert, John Donne, Ben Jonson, John Milton, Henry Vaughan, John Dryden, William Blake, William Wordsworth, Samuel Taylor Coleridge, Alfred Tennyson, Elizabeth Barrett Browning, Christina Rossetti, and Gerard Manley Hopkins. This list does not represent a literary subculture; it constituted—until the late nineteenth century—the tradition itself.

Yet it is misleading to speak of a single tradition of Christian verse, because this vast literary and religious enterprise took many forms—the philosophical speculations of Wordsworth and Tennyson, the supernatural epics of Milton and Blake, the existential lyrics of Donne and Hopkins, and the great congregational hymns of Isaac Watts and William Cowper. At the center of these spiritual traditions, however, stood devotional verse—poetry written to serve as meditations for the spiritual exercises that constitute an important part of Christian religious life.

Devotional verse has always played a significant role in Christian practice, though congregations customarily think of the texts less as poetic than liturgical. Much of the Old Testament is written in verse, and this poetry is ubiquitous in Catholic liturgy, including both the Mass and Divine Office. Monastic worship centers on communal chanting of the Psalms. The many manuals of devotionals, therefore, almost inevitably include Biblical verse in their daily selections. Literary devotional poetry seeks to create new verse to aid the spiritual needs of contemporary believers. The greatest devotional poets in English, such as Herbert and Vaughan, were prolific, writing verse that engaged the reader in every possible spiritual and emotional posture—joy, thanksgiving, anxiety, fear, hope, and sorrow—as well as meditations suitable to the major Christian feasts.

Timothy Murphy's *Devotions* revives this major but neglected poetic genre with variety and amplitude. In over two hundred short poems, Murphy explores the vicissitudes of modern spiritual life. Some of the poems are inspirational, celebrating the joyous mysteries of faith. Others confront the sorrows and failures of contemporary life—presenting unvarnished the painful dramas of sin, despair, repentance, and redemption. Murphy celebrates the saints, but he has not forgotten "the battered, the drunkards, the sinners," among whom the poet numbers himself. In these poems the drama of redemption is not abstract but personal.

The great tradition of devotional verse in English has mostly been Protestant. Among the "Metaphysicals," only Richard Crashaw was Catholic (though John Donne was raised in the Church of Rome). Consequently, the inwardness and individual focus of Calvinism shaped the forms of these devotions. While Murphy sometimes meditates on the solitary soul before God, he characteristically sees Christianity from a Catholic perspective. For him, Christianity is primarily a mystical community, composed of both the living and the dead united by Christ through the sacraments. His themes, though sacred, are remarkably diverse. The book contains meditations on the Psalms, sacraments, major feast days, priesthood, saints, and the daily sacrifice of the Mass. There are even some comic poems for those who forget how Jesus was not above instructing his apostles through humor. *Devotions* is a brave book that recaptures a legacy that has nourished both worship and literature. These are genuine poems rooted in a passionate encounter with the divine. I predict they will find many devoted readers.

—Dana Gioia
Past Chairman of the National Endowment of the Arts
Author of *99 Poems: New and Selected*

I. Companions Met Along the Way

Disenchantment Bay

Touch and go. Our Cessna bumped the sand,
        thumped its tundra tires,
        lifted as if on wires,
banked over ice and rocked its wings to land.

We pitched our camp hard by the Hubbard's face,
        some sixty fathoms tall,
        a seven-mile-long wall
seven leagues from Yakutat, our base.

Crack! A blue serac tottered and gave.
        Stunned at the water's edge,
        we fled our vantage ledge
like oystercatchers skittering from a wave.

Now separation has become my fear.
        What was does not console,
        what is, is past control—
the disembodiment that looms so near.

Detachment? So an ice cliff by the sea
        calves with a seismic crash
        of bergy bits and brash,
choking a waterway with its debris.

We clear the neap tide beach of glacial wrack,
        pace and mark the ground,
        then wave the Cessna round.
Pilot, we bank on you to bear us back.

Liferaft

At Pentecost our guest was Father Hughes.
"Suppose that cancer spreads incurably
through one from whom you cannot bear to part.

Devoted spouse, can you accept this news
with some measure of equanimity?
Have you the Holy Spirit in your heart?"

What steered me there that day, what made him choose
a homily for my own misery?
A mariner needs a sextant, compass, chart.

Nine Bells

God in His mercy gave
the heavens as a clock
to sailors he would save.

Driven by wind and wave,
I steer for Peter's rock
and moor within his nave,

seeking the faith to brave
my first mate in a smock
and sawbones looking grave.

Buoyed Home

The rolling swell
tolls a sinners' bell
that manifests a shoal.

Green and red
flashing far ahead
will guide me to my goal.

I hope to glide
ghosting with the tide
and moor behind the mole.

A nodding nun
wards my shoreward run
but cannot shrive my soul.

Wind River Justice

Alan riding his first horse from Big Sandy
to celebrate his thirty-seventh birthday:
his mare reared in the lodgepoles when a spruce grouse
flushed and nearly pitched him down a switchback.
My own gelding stampeded through a meadow,
and our young wrangler called those ponies "gentled."

We braved Pyramid's boulders, Barnard's clinkers,
apogees of our climbs in the Wind Rivers,
then turned our backs forever on those summits,
Gannet, the tallest peak in all Wyoming,
the Highline Trail cleavered between the Temples.
We limped, blistered, back to our dusty Bronco.

There stood a girl, sobbing beside the stables.
The boy, his terror turned to helpless fury,
and a young ranger argued mixed-use forest,
treeline grazing, lamb-eating bears and coyotes,
leash law and the permitted use of rifles.
Read the rules posted at every entrance.

Two hikers had surprised the sheep at twilight,
young *Lykos* growled, then raced across a meadow
three thousand feet above Big Sandy Trailhead,
and a Basque herder shot the German shepherd
which met no blue heeler or border collie,
no, only a rifle. Wind River Justice.

Bernie Kelly sadly saddled his horses.
Bearers rode up, and *Lykos* down the mountain,
but who descends it twenty-three years later,
no longer carrying Murphy or a backpack?
Slippery the scree, the pool below unfathomed.
Where is the meadow and the watchful shepherd?

Mission Church

I dream that you set forth for Buffalo
just as the blizzard winds begin to blow.
A patch of black ice and a crosswind pitch
your little Chevy nosedown in the ditch.
The nearest farm is only half a mile,
but you lie down half way, to sleep a while.

When the day yawns, you waken stiff but warm,
unscathed by that ferocity of storm
whose windchills fell to fifty-five below.
The cornice where you curled, waiting your tow?
No ninth circle prey to traitorous weather—
that snowflake on your cassock? Gabriel's feather.

Broken Connection

for Helen Hecht

I've known other widows to do just this,
to leave a voice, the tone, the background hiss
on a machine the husband cannot answer.
Telephone tag. Voicemail from a dancer
whose final decade was a sarabande,
the stately wave of a magician's wand.
Missing that voice, I dial his number still.
I hope we will talk again. I pray we will.

Mato Paha

for Joseph Bottum

Like an emergent moth,
I'm flitting up a slope.
Here strips of colored cloth
affixed to every tree
are prayers, the windblown hope
of those who climb to see.

This is a *laccolith*
upthrust through sediment,
perduring like a myth
through man's prehistory,
Pa Sapa's pediment.
Come climb Bear Butte with me.

Twelve hundred feet in dream
I climb when hope is gone,
when like Red Cloud I seem
ringed by my enemies,
when I have need at dawn
for prayer flags in the trees.

Agnóstica

"Is it harder to pray in rhyme or rhyme in prayer?"
asked a great lady, who led me up a stair
to a tall tower, climbed by John of the Cross,
who succored my dear Latina through every loss
which might have cast her soul into despair.
And who were there? Christ, John of the Cross,
a lady who prayed in rhyme and rhymed in prayer.

Prayer for the Virtuous Pagans

My Lord, let me begin with David Miller
whose eldest son is now a pillar
of your temple and your priest,
whose younger sons are battling with the Beast.
Let David behold your face.

And Lord I pray for my own father,
pray too for my little brother,
my sisters and my mother
who lack your sacramental grace.
May all my heathen kin behold your face.

And while I'm here I'll ask another favor.
Mi poetisa whom you savor
because she channels St. John of the Cross,
and in her writing balances each loss
with gain earned in a sonnet's measured space,
may *You* behold *mi Divina Rhina's* face.

David

For the slow death of his father,
the near loss of his mother
and swift death of his brother,
I have a friend who suffers.

An innocent in the Garden,
he shouldered every burden
and marched straight out of Eden
when the angel told him "Go."

He cannot hear the Gospel.
Moses and the Epistles
are no aid in his struggles.
He flees from the Father.

To me he is a beacon
of decency and reason.
Someday the Lord will beckon,
but will David turn home?

Lealty

In a small country graveyard
I watched a man past ninety
crossing himself and kneeling
before a tilted headstone.
I saw he was a farmer
by his Carhartt coverall
and wondered at his stature
unbowed by work or weather.
After he planted flowers
I glanced at the engraving
from Nineteen Twenty-seven
to "Beloved Wife, Maria"
and an infant son, Jason.
The clan name was Chisholm;
their tartan clad my forebears.
What drove them from the Highlands
to our Red River Valley—
hardly a plot in heaven
and half the world from Scotland?
I'll never know their story.

Historian

Leviticus was parroted by Paul,
and the gays lay with Jews in Nazi graves.
    Men would be whipping slaves
if we were wholly in the Bible's thrall.

Your photo on an old dust jacket fades.
Strangers who envied you your boyish looks
    took comfort from your books;
your students grieved when you were felled by AIDS.

John Boswell, you have gone to your long home
where the streets are paved not with gold but dirt
    and the Lord's loins are girt
not with the purple of imperious Rome.

Cast a Cold Eye

Some gays decide "I'm called to be a priest."
Some farm, Antaeans rooted in the soil,
others turn to the arts, thinking "At least
I won't be shuffling off this mortal coil
quietly." No, they leave some trace behind,
a chapel ceiling, a volume on a shelf,
passionate proof that God centered the mind
on something larger than one's sorry self.

Twice I refused the siren call of Rome.
Domine non sum dignus. And the farm?
Betting badly I forfeited my home,
caused my partners irreparable harm,
and forty years have taught me I confuse
the Holy Spirit with a drunken muse.

To the Dean

I was amazed to see *Batter my heart*
in the breviary of a Catholic priest
who wages battle with The Beast
and longs to divine your art.

You make it look so easy, Dr. Donne:
from courtier to prelate in a minute
timed by the human heartbeats in it,
a sprint to heaven won.

I am the much indebted legatee
of lines four hundred years have not erased,
your ardent lover, never chaste
except you ravish me.

God was the sitting judge for your complaint.
Amice curiae, win for me relief
from mortal sin as though my brief
were argued by a saint.

Sub-Zero

The night is clear. Stars of the northern skies
fly overhead like millions of mayflies
or star-nosed moles. Fenian pokes his nose
in every alpha marking in the snows,
and Stephen Edgar, walking, takes a fall,
a small catastrophe, Stephen is so tall.

I hoist him to his feet and brush the snow
from dustcoats. It is thirty-three below.
I limp him in and park him by the fire,
pour him a brandy and put on a choir.
Of course all of this happened in a dream.
Eight thousand miles are not all that they seem.

How did you start, Stephen? With Dylan Thomas?
Who was the wellspring of your poet's promise?
Was it a woman? Was it a buttoned bodice
when fumbling fingers first essayed the goddess?
Promise me this. After our race is run,
you'll introduce me to your friend, John Donne.

Father Peter

Good Friday, and the church was draped in black.
He'd borne a massive cross up to the altar.
Despite his slender frame he didn't falter,
and his voice carried forcefully to the back:

"I tell an unwed girl 'Thou shalt not kill,'
and the next morning I anoint the dying.
Our unemployed have hungry infants crying;
our uninsured can't pay the doctor's bill.

Only six months ago I was ordained
to bear you witness and console your loss,
to suffer with each victim on his cross—
tasks for which a priest is called, not trained."

Fearing the chosen of the Lord are few,
I knelt unshriven in the sinners' pew.

The Parsonage

Far from the madding crowd's ignoble strife
—Thomas Gray

Helping the faithful battle their despair,
he lives alone in his broad-shouldered house.
He vowed to God he'd never take a spouse,
and now three hundred wives are in his care.
Who to marry and bury them but he,
and none but Christ to keep him company?

His is the only intellect in town
to ferret errors from the Septuagint.
Hebrew, Latin, and Greek he learnt by dint
of midnight toil that won him no renown.
Keyboard and screen are his scriptorium,
ad maiorem Dei gloriam.

He heats canned soup. The housekeeper just died.
She never made her pilgrimage to Rome,
never returned to County Cork, her home.
But praise the Lord, she is her Savior's bride.
He thinks "I now pronounce you God and wife."
His is a busy, solitary life.

Dakota Virtues

Out here we still pray at our forebears' graves,
and quilting is esteemed among the arts.
The handshake is a contract in these parts,
and most of us believe that Jesus saves.

The Runner

A frosty dawn: it isn't even seven.
I pass a hooded jogger on the walk.
Father? A sidelong grin, no time for talk.
My priest is on his daily race to heaven.

To Jason

Solitary confinement with your tears?
If hope and love elude you, live in dread
of what awaits your killer when you're dead:
grief measured in eons, not in years.

Grace Notes

What is the garland briefer than a girl's?
Well I know one, that of the boy soprano
who girds his little loins and combs his curls
to sing King David by a grand piano.

The Transplant

for Danny Mahli

We stalk the ruins of a former farm
for mushrooms, search the base of every tree.
Blackflies, mosquitoes and no-see-ums swarm,
and a wood tick is creeping up my knee.

Back at the truck, we soak a dingy towel
to wrap the tap root of an infant oak
dug from the Sand Hills with a sharpened trowel.
High overhead we hear a raven croak.

Danny, I held your infants in my arms,
"*Ego vos baptizo*," I softly said.
The spirit trees come from our forebears' farms
where leaves speak their sibilants to the dead.

Psalm 139

"Three flaws, but this comes very near your best."
I bent to work, wrestling with all his points,
a student taking a professor's test,
an acolyte a cardinal anoints?

Three nights after my failing father died
its author faxed "The Darkness and the Light."
I read it to my mother, and the stride
of trimeter carried us both that night.

"You know, you're young enough to be my son,"
lies in my secret trove of treasured letters.
He thought me young when I was fifty-one
and liked the verses written to my betters.

"He can't see you, he's too ill to get dressed,"
his wife, so soon a grieving widow, said.
Propped on a cane, he'd looked his bow-tied best.
I would have gone and knelt beside his bed.

Darkness dims nothing for you:
Night shines forth as day.
For you the two are alike,
The darkness and the light.

The quatrain from 139 is from the new Alan Sullivan translation,
The Psalms of King David.

Footsore

"Tough as the leather on a Red Wing boot"
—so Steve, on Alan's tolerance for pain.
Though drugs and radiation dull his brain,
today he calls himself "A well-armed coot."
He's bought a new support, a cherry cane.

Cherry is hardwood, and the handle bent
into a shepherd crook around the shaft
has so much heft our cancer victim laughed,
"The staff of Moses from Mount Sinai sent?
Carving and carpentry? My savior's craft!"

Grant us the courage, Lord, to cope with loss
when strength deserts us as it drains from him.
There is a stream that every soul must swim
after it walks the Stations of the Cross.

Our Thirty-Seventh Pentecost

This is doubly our anniversary:
five years ago your cancer was diagnosed.
Tonight I'll kneel to pray a Rosary
and offer homage to the Holy Ghost
who brought two boys together long ago,
steering us to the high plains from the sea,
condemning you to decades in the snow,
me to subarctic darkness of the soul.
Our westward road entailed a heavy toll.

"Like to a lamp that shines in a dark place"
the morning star rose in my heart, then yours.
For one condemned to death, the state of grace
is blinding as the cornered spirit soars
like a sage grouse flushing from bitterbrush
or rabbit bush, seeking the sun's embrace,
primaries pumping in a frantic rush.
We both thirst for a waterhole, where calm
grants to the heart the solace of a psalm.

Interment

One boy with a guitar and dreadful novel,
another, poems crammed inside his head—
one led the other to his basement hovel
and slung the slender stranger into bed.

They would find seven hundred trees to tend
and eighteen types of apples to be grafted,
dogs to be fed and watered, and God send
the manuscripts of poems to be crafted.

So it went on for decades, so we grow,
but now one digs beside two teenage trees,
acorns unearthed, transplanted years ago,
slim oaks, leaves yellowed by last night's freeze.

I delve a deep hole in the orchard soil,
singing my lover's favorite Latin song,
Tantum Ergo. The digging is no toil.
My friend? Let me pretend he did no wrong.

Alan's Ashes

I. *In Extremis*

From that first Pentecost we had been told
multiple cancers would lay waste to you.
You asked I read you David, who was new
to one God wouldn't suffer to grow old.
He sought a servant for the holy fire
and needing a new tenor for His choir
He brought you to the altar and the pew.
You were seduced at Christmas. Eastertide
He moved you, poet, to a work of thanks
for exiting the unbelievers' ranks.
Humbly you became our Savior's bride
and slaved in Egypt's mines to make anew
King David's poems, of which we have too few.
Offered a choice, you took the angels' side.

II. Artists' Hill

This is the Wilbur plot on Artists' Hill,
the spade so worn, a torture to the hands
of him who wields it if he wears no gloves.
Richard has reached the age of eighty-seven.
Charlee and Laurie have escaped to heaven,
but two holes must be dug, an old friend's loves
buried in ground where ashes sleep until
the trumpet sounds, and bodies rise from sands
or deep loam where they sleep. So Alan stakes
the ground as weeds head in the field edge rows;
over our heads mosquitoes hum, and crows
intone their interest in the dead. Alan takes
the spade in hand, still strong but chemo-slim.
The next hole to be dug I'll dig for him.

III. The Ashes

I feared the US Postal Service lost
your ashes which arrived here just today,
eleven days via "Priority Mail,"
the final sea on which you set your sail
only to have your ashes float astray,
shipped and returned, delivered double-crossed.
Now what to do? A consecrated plot,
a granite headstone bearing both our names
without my year of death? That will come soon
measured by the swift transits of the moon.
I thank Michael the Archangel who tames
my grief when I'm self-pitying my lot.
Live on, *mon vieux*, in words you sometimes wrote
when Jesus seized his servant by the throat.

IV. Court of Honor

In dream I sit, holding your unbound books.
Scouts and scoutmasters cast me sidelong looks
as though to say "Your mate has met his end,
forget him." Then an advocate and friend,
a face from boyhood, from Camp Wilderness,
strides from the crowd to tidy up my mess
of loose leaf papers in an ordered stack.

Wings flexed by the muscles on his back,
he soars above our council fire, our rings
of split-log seats, and cries "King David *sings*."
The scouts are stunned. I speak from memory
Psalms Two and Eight, your Psalm One Thirty-three,
lyrics translated for an English choir
of boy sopranos warmed around a fire.

II. From Camp Wilderness to Prairie St. John's Hospital

Agapē

The night you died, I dreamed you came to camp
to hear confession from an Eagle scout
tortured by forty years of sin and doubt.
You whispered Vespers by a hissing lamp.

Handlers, allowing you to hike with me,
followed us to the Bad Axe waterfront
down a firebreak this camper used to hunt.
Through all I said you suffered silently.

I blamed the authors of my unbelief:
St. Paul, who would have deemed my love obscene,
the Jesuit who raped me as a teen,
the altar boy when I was six, the grief

of a child chucked from Eden, left for dead
by Peter's Church and all the choirs above.
In a thick Polish accent choked with love,
Te Dominus amat was all you said.

Father Jack

A diamond willow grew beside a brook,
roots undercut, bending above the bank.
Carefully carved, it made a shepherd's crook
for one who sorrowed at a bully's prank.

He stoked the campfires as his charges slept
and the dreamt bear crept from its forest cave.
Comforting the youngest when they wept,
tousling their heads, he said "A Scout is brave."

Why he renounced his vows no one can say.
Certainly not for leading boys astray.

The Axe Head

My cedar bit was balanced for a boy
who weighed one thirty, stood near five eleven.
Too broad for oak, the right tool to deploy
on pine and aspen, mine was the axe of heaven.

I notched new fence rails for our firing range
and once felled eight white pines in half an hour,
young trees, eight-inchers, thought it rich and strange
to lop and lash them for a signal tower.

To Tenderfeet, I taught compass and map,
then dropped a jack pine on a driven stake,
taught constellations. Not for me the slap
of taut tummies flopping on Bad Axe Lake.

It was the woods, it was the hills for me,
Christ crucified, the spirit in every tree.

Cross-lashed

A chapel, not a church:
just a clearing in the wood
of aspen, pine and birch,
where a rude altar stood

pegged by a boy's hands;
behind it a birchwood cross
cross-lashed, but neither stands.
They are gone under the moss.

When I quit Wilderness Camp
I rose up from my knees
and left the altar lamp
burning in the trees.

Summits would loom above
the stony trails I trod.
Sex led me to love;
love bound me to God.

The Bowline

A young sailor plummeted from a tree.
Stunned as though a spreader had cracked his head,
he lay six months unmoving, nearly dead.
To rouse him from insensibility
a wise doctor gave him a length of rope,
said "Bowline." The rabbit popped up the hole,
and hopped counter-clockwise around the bole.
Prayers had been heard, a mooring made for hope.

Survivor

I never bought that Magnum .44.
I had my .410 pistol, single shot.
Sure, it could blow my brains out, like as not,
but bankers, lawyers? I don't go to war.

Three years of patient psychotherapy
cured me of murder—others or myself—
and sent me to some textbooks on my shelf:
the Tao Te Ching, King David spoke to me.

Dr. Kolotkin walked me past my past:
rage at my father, rage at the Catholic Church
which leaves every gay boy in the lurch
of bigotry, embittered and outcast.

The peace I found stays with me to this day.
Gun under my pillow, I kneel and pray.

Prison Chaplain

for Stuart Longtin

Heavy and gray now, dressed in deacon's robes—
I see you in your Speedo at Floyd Lake,
its nylon clinging to those golden globes
you exercised for Moorhead football's sake.

We hiked the Black Trail to Itasca Park,
but now I see a deacon hard at work
explicating the Gospel of St. Mark,
our high school quarterback become a clerk—

in the high sense. A boy with such good looks,
you could have run to Hollywood and whored
but turned to mastery of sacred books
and the manly mimesis of our Lord.

Lifesaver, that was your job at Wilderness,
teaching tenderfoot farm boys how to swim.
Soulsaver, I would call you now and bless
any man who preaches Saint Mark to Tim.

We take our coffee outside for the view,
patrol the walk-about with twelve-foot mesh
where drunks can smoke. What has become of Stu?
The Word. Not on the page but in the flesh.

—*Prairie St. John's Hospital*

"Arise."

The stitches near his chin,
the wrong part of his neck,
a bad jab by a wreck:
the boy so tall, so thin,

not knowing when to kneel,
not knowing where to thrust
the knife, no one to trust,
no house in which to heal.

I'm sober here today
where I've been drunk before,
where staff lock every door
and children stay away.

I'm called here by a dove
to say the word Christ said
to Lazarus, four days dead
and waiting for God's love.

—*Prairie St. John's Hospital*

Hospital Chaplain

to Father Jose Mundadan

I failed you once, the Adolescent Floor,
where those who die, who knows if they are missed?
How often have the children there been kissed?
That was no place for one with no degree
in medicine or in psychology.
Nurses, big women, warded every door.
Bandages guarded every other wrist.

—*Prairie St. John's Hospital*

Sunshine in the Morning

Sister Marie was strolling up the sidewalk,
munching a raw potato. Many inmates
watched from our fenced enclosure, bleakly smoking.
Sister Marie, between bites of potato,
wimpled and radiant in her brown habit,
sang in her fog-horn voice *Salve Regina*.
Blue-eyed Corinne, enslaved to oxycodone,
said "Whatever she's on, I want to have it."

—*Prairie St. John's Hospital*

The Second Step

We came to believe that a power greater than ourselves
could restore us to sanity. – *The Big Book*

I. For Rich or for Poor

Four thousand acres, every parcel squared—
a river oxbowed through it, and its beds
drained it of torrents every summer sheds,
and there never a prairie rose was spared.

The day we met Ed glared up at my chin
and scoffed at my pretensions. "Boy, your bank
holds you in hock. Where do you think you rank?
You're just a worm of Eve conceived in sin."

Spindly I thought it, wheat sick in the dust.
"Wheat? This is bluegrass in its second year,
and every bushel here is free and clear
and six Kentucky dollars I can trust."

I watched a hand herd cattle. "Is that Dan?"
"Pay no mind to my son. He's just a drunk,"
but decades later, when their farm is sunk,
I search out Dan, survivor of his clan,

to ask for help. All Ed's vast fortune gone
is nothing to the little girl Dan lost.
And thirty million dollars? Trifling cost,
notes swept by a whirlwind from a lawn.

Will he befriend an Irishman who seeks
to marry abstinence and piety?
We are both bankrupt, but sobriety—
Dan measures it in decades, I in weeks.

II. Two Poets

Mikey's idea of going on the wagon
was sorrowfully to pour that final flagon
of single malt whiskey down the drain,
then switch to marijuana and cocaine.

He simply couldn't comprehend the danger
of drying out. Although he was no stranger
to white knuckling the vomit and the shakes,
he didn't know he gamed for mortal stakes.

Three times I have been felled by lightning pain
as seizures short-circuited my brain.
Three times, waking in hospital at dawn
all memory of my repertoire was gone,

and once I'd nearly bitten through my tongue.
Let me leave self-destruction to the young
who need not fear, not yet, the fatal stroke
that lifted from my friend addiction's yoke.

III. My Mentor

Wallwork could be the soberest man on earth
except that he was wasted half the time,
able to give a million, shave a dime.
Money was central to his sense of worth.

Should not have been the case. Harvard degree,
intellect incandescent in the extreme,
a trophy wife, a life lived in a dream
turned nightmare for its want of sanctity.

Wallwork was an enabler for me,
forcefully putting forth his monied power
to finance mortgaged farms where I could glower,
blind to my growing inebriety.

I have loved men divorced from heaven's grace
for whom, fraying my jeans, I nightly pray
and earn indulgences on All Souls' Day.
Of Wallwork and my poet friend I say
"Embrace them Lord, let them behold Your face."

IV. *In Absentia*

Waking at seven? I should be at my meeting,
sober as any lawyer, any plumber.
Tonight I had signed up to do the greeting,
to search the hopeless eyes of each newcomer
and say to him, "Nobody here is flawless.
We have twelve laws, and all of us were lawless."

Prayer for Sobriety

Morning glories climbing the garden wall
vie with the fragrant jasmine to outshine
the sun emerging from a summer squall.
Blossom and vine, lover and love entwine.
He is the Groom, and I? The shy betrothed
enraptured by the faith I so long loathed.

This is the sacramental cup we drink,
this the unleavened loaf on which we dine,
deliverance from the sins to which I sink.
Here is the book, the work of my Divine
Redeemer at whose Word the worlds revolve.
Let me return His passion with resolve.

—*Prairie St. John's Hospital*

III. Whoso List to Hunt

Hunter's Grace

For the crops in our fields,
for the cocks in our crops,
good dogs, straight shooting,
we thank thee, great God.

Poacher

The king's deer graze the green,
meat for the village feasts.
The Lord says "Rule the beasts."

Tonight the moon is full
and short, the bowstring's pull.

"Rise Peter; kill, and eat"
—words of the Paraclete
in Acts X:13.

Perro del Amo

Go where the blue wings flash
over the whitecapped wave,

where crippled mallards splash
and every bitch is brave.

When the returning dove
roosts at your mother's grave,

I'll bury a box of ash
beside her in the sod.

Vaya con Dios, love,
you were the dog of God.

Huntress

for Dan Treat, DVM

Her first bird was a crippled mourning dove.
  She somersaulted down a ditch
    head over heels in love,
buttoned her bird and bounded up the pitch.

Her first drake dropped beyond a refuge sign.
  Wriggling under the lowest wire,
    she swam a perfect line
as though posting a proof of her desire.

Her first goose gave her nose a nasty peck.
  Battered by its unbroken wing
    she leapt to grab its neck
and growling, dragged it back for me to wring.

Her first loss was her superhuman ear.
  Hand-signaled on each unmarked run,
    she could no longer hear
whistling wingtips; even at last, the gun.

At fourteen she was walking into walls,
  fouling the carpet, losing teeth.
    Farewell to mallard calls
and decoy spreads, wild roosters on the heath.

To St. Francis of Fargo fell the chore,
  the Nembutol a gentle thrust
    to launch her from our shore.
The last look in her fearless eye was trust.

Checklist

Cheetos and chocolate chips for Tim to nibble,
a shrink-wrapped pound of Jimmy's jerkied deer,
a six-pack of nonalcoholic beer,
for Feeney's sake a Ziplock bag of kibble,

my Thompson .410 pistol underneath
the driver's seat; towrope and jumper cables,
the Game and Fish sunrise and sunset tables,
my lockback Buck knife in its buckskin sheath,

Nitro Solvent, Rem Oil and cleaning rod,
boxes of Super X non-toxic shot—
can there be anything that I forgot?
The truck is packed. The luck I leave to God.

Faith

Two dozen shells to harvest just three birds?
It was the vilest shooting of my life,
unspeakable in Anglo-Saxon words.
Better, had I just thrown my Boy Scout knife.
The Father taketh and the Spirit giveth,
but me? I know that my Retriever liveth.

Missing Mass

He hath put a new song in my mouth.
Psalm 40:3

Going to church afield,
I bear the Decalogue
as St. Michael, his shield.
My faithful altar dog
precedes me up the aisle,
mile after dusty mile.

A gale sweeps through the choir
and dries the prostrate grass
lightning and prairie fire
forge to beaten brass.
Tinted anew each day,
the dome is blue or gray.

Hearing the Psalmist's call,
the blood of every bird
sacrificed this fall
I translate into Word.
Responsive, I record
a new song to the Lord.

Ecce Canis

From the first slough some forty birds flushed wild.
      Maddened by pheasant scent,
      Bold Fenian was with child
while I triangulated where they went.

North to the mallards' frozen mating hole,
      a second cattail slough
      rimming a bullrush bowl,
we hunted, panting as the pheasants flew,

all but their patriarch who fell stone dead.
      I watched his grandson go,
      a gutshot cock that sped
to switchgrass tufted in the distant snow.

Under those drifts our harder hunt began.
      Eluding every cast,
      it burrowed, bolted, ran
until at last Fenian pinned it fast.

I floundered to a roadside willow stand,
      collapsing on a log
      where Feeney licked my hand.
Unworthy man, behold thy hunting dog.

Soul of the North

Out of the wilds, I pray.
Bound by my northern birth
to fish, to hunt the earth
and follow my forebears' way,
I mutter *I have sinned*,
wander the knee-high grass,
flourish awhile and pass
whistling into the wind.

As char swim to the clear
tundra rivers that run
under the midnight sun,
as wolves follow the deer
drawn from ford to ford,
as clamorous geese in V's
throng to the thawing seas—
all creatures of one accord—
my soul thirsts for the Lord.

Consolation

Fenian, you winded your favorite smell,
    crashing through chest-high brush
    in falling snow, to flush
two cocks my stuck safety has saved from Hell.

"Kennel!" I hide a warm bird in the sod,
    staging a blind retrieve
    in which you so believe,
my whistle signals seem the Word of God.

Harvest Moon

A year ago Steve saw me in seizure's throes
and told his wife he'd bidden goodbye to Tim.
Frank Miller gave me the last rites, and Frank knows,
Christ's priest that he is, when eyes go dim,
pulse slows, blue takes the fingers and the toes,
pray for the soul.
                                        Tonight a full moon rose
and sang over my head a harvest hymn.

Hunting on Thanksgiving

for Steve Syrdal

Thanks for my tall, Norwegian hunting buddy.
I love him best when his right hand is bloody
from gutting birds; and thanks too, for the true
friend you found me when I was twenty-two.
He flees from me, but I attach no blame
to Alan, who would never clean my game.

Thanks for the dog who frolics as I slog,
mud to my ankles, through this flooded bog.
Thanks for the pheasant stuffed into my vest
whose felling in these weeds was just a test
of heart pounding and fouled lungs out of breath,
for Father Frank, who will attend my death.

Thanks for the bird I missed, for Feeney's flush,
the faint thunder of wings breaking the hush
of mass conducted in the open air.
Thanks for pulling me back from the despair
that might have lost me eighteen hundred days
I have devoted to my Maker's praise.

Syrdal

I have a brother who's no blood of mine
except, perhaps, back in the Viking days.
Nobody else so passionately prays
I'll play my minor part in God's design.

He's never smoked, never drunk to excess.
Inches taller and years shorter than I,
two times he saw me such a sodden mess
he told his wife "I think Tim's going to die."

Ranging afield for years with dog and gun
we forged a bond that is unbreakable,
and certain as the rising of the sun
we share a faith that is unshakeable.

Samaritan, he found me in a ditch.
With that which matters most I am most rich.

Posted

Drive with caution. This township strip of gravel
is much impeded by a herd of pheasants
    flaunting their adolescence,
and it is posted thus: Restricted Travel.

Beside me is an unmowed stretch of meadow
Feeney and I were tempted by all summer.
    One month hence some Hummer
will cast over this grass its massive shadow

as herds of Fargo bankers, lawyers, brokers,
who have shelled out their seven hundred dollars
    on GPS collars
which pointers wear like diamond-studded chokers,

hunt on this land I once farmed to perdition.
God bless the rich. I was one and I know ’em
    and say to them this poem
without a hint of malice or sedition:

Feeney and I shall walk and flush some pheasants,
strolling without our double-barreled Browning,
    the one of us not clowning
awed in September by an August presence.

Fathers' Day

Sunset, and mallards poured down on the pond.
You shot from a low saddle in the hills,
felling them like a wizard with his wand
while I was wading to retrieve your kills.
Father, ten years have passed since you expired,
six children at your bedside, eighty-three,
stricken by angina each time you tired.

Our young priest speaks a handsome homily
on God the Father and the Son he gave
to save this sorry world. We're told to pray
for every father resting in his grave,
for each child who is fatherless today.

Prayer to St. Michael

Through tree rows flanked by harvested corn
where Gabriel winds his hunting horn,
through cattail sloughs where pups rejoice
with ardent boys, let me give voice
like a hound hot on the scent of a fox
to the art of hunting pheasant cocks
through wild grasses ungrazed by cattle.
Michael the Archangel, lead us in battle.

When farmers are finishing up their toil
and ploughs turn over the stubbled soil,
when whitetail bucks commence their rut
and squirrels are squirreling every nut,
when acorns fall from the scrub oak trees
and sunrise wakens the northwest breeze,
when leaves and limbs begin to rattle,
Michael the Archangel, lead us in battle.

Where hoar frost silvers the unhayed grass
and zigzag lines mark every pass,
where ringnecks tunnel out of view
and mallard wings are fringed with blue
and the doe sleeps in a switchgrass bed,
where green is gold, the reddest red
is Thomas Turkey's impressive wattle.
Michael the Archangel, lead us in battle.

from The Chase

December 15
I pick my slow way past the pockmarked sedge
        where calves have kicked their divots,
then climb to hunt the upland's grassy edge
        rounding the center pivots
    whose verdant verge I choose to stalk.
There breakfast lies within a rooster's walk.

The prairie is a poem rarely read.
        Its looseleaf pages blow.
Too many students of this landscape fled
        its poverty and snow.
    Today I limp on stiffening knees,
hoping that heedless pheasants take their ease

in pigeon grasses sprung from durum stubble,
        in fragrant cedar shadow
where a boy watched his father down a double.
        Maker of marsh and meadow,
    grant me more time to understand,
more years to walk and memorize this land.

IV. In David's Line

I've no faith in the power of my prayer.
Grant me the grace to phrase
a song of thanks and praise
from one who lists among his sins despair.

Psalm 42

As the doe pants for the running brook
my soul thirsts for the Lord.

It thirsts for my God, the living
God; when will I come
and see the face of the Lord?

Bread to me night and day,
my tears constantly say:
    "Where is your God?"

Remembering, I pour forth
my soul: a multitude
had passed to the house of God,
all of us voicing joy and praise
and keeping his holy days.

Why are you, my soul,
cast down, disconsolate?
Hope in the Lord, for I
shall praise my deliverance,
the light of my countenance,
    my God.

My soul, cast down, remembers
my Lord in the land of Jordan,
Hermon, the mount of Mizar.

Abyss calls to abyss
at the sound of your cataracts.
Breakers, waves overwhelm me.

By day the Lord my God
mandates his loving mercy.
At night his song is with me,
my prayer to the God of my life.

I will say to God my rock
"Why have you forgotten me?
Why do I go in mourning,
oppressed by my enemies?

As though breaking my bones
my enemies reproached me,
asking me every day:
"Where is your God?"

Why are you, my soul,
cast down, disconsolate?
Hope in the Lord, for I
shall praise my deliverance,
the light of my countenance,
my God.

Psalm 137

attributed to Jeremiah in the time of captivity

By the rivers of Babylon
we sat down and wept
as we remembered Zion.

We hung our harps
on willows in their midst.

Our captors asked for a song,
tormentors demanding:
"Sing us a song of Zion."

How shall we sing the Lord's
song in an alien land?

If I forget you
Jerusalem,
let my right hand forget,

if I fail to recall you
let my tongue cleave
to the roof of my mouth—
if I fail to raise Jerusalem
above my greatest gladness.

Recall O Lord
Edom's children
in the day of Jerusalem,
who said "Raze her! Raze her
to her foundation stones."

Daughter of Babylon
to be destroyed,
happy is he who requites you
as we were recompensed.

Happy is he who dashes
your infants against the stones.

The Sentry's Psalm (130)

for Boaz and Tzur Zohar

Out of the depths I cry to you, Lord.

Hear my voice, my supplications.
O Lord, were you to retain our sins,
who could remain upright?

With you there is forgiveness,
thus we hold you in awe.

I wait for the Lord, my soul awaits,
I hope in the word of the Lord.

My soul waits for the Lord
as do we on watch until morning,
more than we who watch for the morning.

Israel, hope in the Lord,
with him are pity and ransom.

He will redeem Israel
from its iniquities.

Psalm 98

Sing a new song to the Lord
for the marvels that he makes
with his right hand; his arm
is our deliverance.

To us he shows salvation;
to the Gentiles' eyes, justice.

He calls to mind his kindness,
his faith to the house of Israel;
so to the ends of the earth
the salvation of God is seen.

Raise a great shout to the Lord,
earth, cry out, sing praises.

Sing to the Lord with a lyre,
a lyre and the sounds of song,

with a trumpet, with a ram's horn
blow a blast for the Lord, our king.

Let the sea rage in its fullness
with the world and all its dwellers.

Let the rivers clap their hands
and the hills sing out together

to the Lord who comes to judge
the earth with righteousness
and the people equably.

The Septuagint
for Seree Cohen Zohar

Seventy-two elders
sequestered by Ptolemy
Philadelphus in chambers,
a cell for every scholar,
were told by the King of Egypt:
"Translate the books of *Moshe*,
your teacher, into Greek."

Two days and ten weeks later
seventy-two translations
transcribed from memory
by gray-bearded *rebbis*
were word for word the same.
When you believe this legend,
you will know the Holy Spirit.

The Reversion

Born to go astray,
I fled the Catholic fold
when I was twelve years old,
a lamb who ran away,
prey to the wolves, the cold.

My shepherd piped me home.
Filing into a pew,
I learned what Caesar knew:
all roads lead to Rome
where wolves are mothers too.

Scaring the Parish

Am I too tattered to pray?
I have scuffed the tips of my shoes
and they are beyond polishing.
I have frayed my blue jeans' knees
and they are beyond patching.
And Lord, my disarray?
It comes of so much kneeling.

Father Tom Leads the Faithful in Prayer

We pray first for our Pope.
Lend him the strength to cope
with those who have no hope.
Lord hear our prayer.

For those ripped from the womb
and buried without a tomb,
for those who wrought their doom—
Lord hear our prayer.

For leaders who betray
their Catholic faith and stray
far from the Truth, the Way—
Lord hear our prayer.

For each who has no faith
and goes through life, a wraith
not knowing what God saith—
Lord hear our prayer.

The poorest of the poor
are knocking at the door.
How can our church do more?
Lord hear our prayer.

For all the faithful dead,
freed from our mortal dread,
who trod the paths we tread—
Lord hear our prayer.

That Michael's blazing sword,
the right arm of the Lord,
lead us to our reward—
Lord hear our prayer.

That God may someday see
this world of misery
as it was meant to be—
  Lord hear our prayer.

Champion

Over the mats he tumbled.
Over the horse he vaulted,
but landing hard he stumbled
and limping off, halted:
the humble shall be exalted
and the exalted, humbled.

II Peter 1:19

One who beheld his face
but played a coward's part
likened him to a light
that shines in a dark place—

much as the morning star,
rising on my black heart,
came at the close of night
and found me from afar.

No Turning Back

Pierce the Eye of the Needle
no caravan can pass.
Ride without a saddle
the white foal of an ass.
A potter will leave his treadle,
a mason gray with grout
kneel to kiss your sandal,
and all the stones cry out.

To the Corinthians

Pistis, elpis, agapē:
what do these Greek words mean?
Elpis throws me a rope
that *pistis* grasps, unseen;
but love in its largest sense,
love in the perfect tense
with which I cannot cope
and cannot dream to copy?
There I repose my hope.

In David's House

51. Asperges me

Cleanse me of my iniquity
and wash away my sins.
Laugh, Lord, at my obliquity.
In you laughter begins.

Regard our little steeples.
You gave to the High Plains
a flock of sheep, the peoples
who drink deep when it rains.

I shall number all the stones
Assyria has laid low.
I shall number all my bones
as David did long ago.

Oh, what a troubled route man took,
descending from the trees:
cave paintings and the printed book
made on his bended knees.

Lord, the broken spirit,
the sorrows in my heart
are much, much to inherit
and hard, hard to impart.

130. De profundis clamavi

Out of the depths I cry,
the fathomless depths of a sea
from which my soul would fly.
Lord, have mercy on me.

A battlement I walk,
and every other turning
faces me east. I balk
and pray, pray for the morning.

33.Cantate ei canticum novum

A new song for the Lord!
Spring comes to Dakota:
give prayers to the adored,
children of the Lakota,

the Rosebud, Lower Brule,
you, your Germanic neighbors,
ring no bell at a school,
no man bend to his labors.

This is your Eastertide,
so leave unsown the furrow.
Your groom waits for his bride,
the corn waits for tomorrow.

22. Diviserunt vestimenta

They cast lots for my vesture
and pierced my hands and feet—
no rhetorical gesture
but Word of the Paraclete,

advocate for our souls,
forgiver of all wrongs
made on the bed of coals
where David forged his songs.

103. Flos agri sic florebit

To every field, a flower.
To every scythe, a pass
where voles and angels cower.
To every gale, the grass.

To the Chief Musician

"Break the teeth in their mouths, Oh Lord," he cried.

We Christians can no longer pray this way
to Him our mortal sins have crucified,
but at our funerals we often say:

"Where shall I find my refuge and hold fast
except under the shadow of Thy wings
until all my calamities are past?"

So from antiquity King David sings.

Sundance

When we were very small and knew no Jews
we asked, "Did Adolf Hitler kill them all?"
Today I dreamt I stood at the Wailing Wall
and slipped a folded prayer between two stones.
I grieved for the incinerated bones,
for Nazi guards who knelt in wooden pews.
I prayed for Medieval Jews at Mainz
chained to the stake and burned by "Christian" hands.

There was a holocaust in my back yard—
the Winchester and Colt versus the bow,
the dazed survivors starving in the snow,
ghost dancers praying for the buffalo's
return to land where grass is all that grows.
Women, children, slain by their mounted guard,
pitched in a mass grave at Wounded Knee—
learning this long ago so sickened me
I bowed where skulls of buffalo were hung
and prayed not to the dead, but for the young.

Winter Wheat

Our prairie views are skewed forever West;
ours is a land of drought and blowing sand,
and any questing eagle can attest
that one must soar to fathom western land.
The sun subsides behind the mountain's chest,
embittered ranchers hoard the Kruggerand,
and last night when I lay down to my rest,
I heard my Father's clarion command:

The word made flesh. I breathed this to Saint John
who stood beside my bride, my own son's cross.
I built you mountains you could climb upon,
and once I even flooded inland seas
where winter wheat now rises to your knees.
You are my child. Do not compound my loss.

To St. Paul on His Feast Day

Reading my congregation your account
of Christ's heavenly light that struck you blind,
I thought God in His mercy seized your mind
and threw one rider from his Hell-bent mount.

Have you no ears to hear nor eyes to see?
Father and Son and Holy Spirit ask us.
Most of us gallop blindly toward Damascus,
goaded by guilt and fleeing Calvary.

To Timothy

Bring me my cloak. Bring Mark.
This prison cell is dark
and Luke, my only friend.
I am very near the end,
nothing much left but bone.
The shackled mastiffs bark,
and other prisoners groan.
Mortal this cold, this dark.
Bring me my cloak. Bring Mark
whom I can lean upon.
And if you find him, John.

Confessiones 10.27.38

Wrongly believing beauty lay without,
   blindly I flailed about.
   How late did I begin
to realize your beauty lay within.
   To one deprived of sight
   you said *Let there be light,*
   and to my deafened ear
you called, you cried! hoping that I might hear.
   I thirsted, hungered, yearned.
   You touched me, and I burned.
   How late I came to you,
Beauty ever ancient, ever new.
   How late I came to you.

—after St. Augustine

Last Words of Beowulf

“I offer my thanks   to the Almighty Master,
the King of Glory,   for granting my kindred
these precious things   I look upon last.
Losing my life,   I have bought this boon
to lighten my leave-day.   Look to our people,
for you shall be leader;   I lead no longer.
Gather my guard   and raise me a grave-mound
housing my ashes   at Hronesnaesse,
reminding my kin   to recall their king
after his pyre   has flared on the point.
Seafarers passing   shall say when they see it
‘Beowulf’s Barrow’   as bright longboats
drive over darkness,   daring the flood.”

So the stern prince   bestowed on his sword-thane
and keen spear-wielder   the kingly collar,
his gold-plated helm   and hammered hauberk.
He told him to bear them   bravely in battle:
“Farewell, Wiglaf,   last Waegmunding.
I follow our fathers,   foredestined to die,
swept off by fate,   though strong and steadfast.”
These heartfelt words   were the warrior’s last
before his body   burned in the bale-fire
and his soul sought   the doom of the truthful.

The Seven

Acedia
A lassitude, mistranslated as Sloth
    by men who wore the cloth,
Acedia is very near despair.
Call it the precondition for my prayer.

Avaritia
For thirty years I schemed to strike it rich,
but I was a false lover, rightly spurned
by *Avaritia*, that greedy bitch.
Hers were not the riches for which I burned.

Invidia
"Desiring this man's art and that man's scope"?
When in despair with Sonnet Twenty-nine
    I all alone repine,
Dante tells me I'm damned. "Abandon hope."

Gula
Aquinas clad in flab—
punishment for a sin
which I am innocent of.
Distance runner thin,
I was no muscled slab—
no Greek with olive skin—
when mastered by the love
where all my dreams begin.

"Such gluttony!" I cry.
But drink? I am unmanned.
Pour me a shot of rye
and still my trembling hand.

Superbia
Pride is the face I put on shame,
    the arrogant refulgence
for which the Lord will strike my name
    from the book of His indulgence.

Luxuria et Ira
What a long way to climb,
bearing so large a load.
Diminishing, the time
left to me is my goad.
Is time itself the climb?

Lust has left me behind.
Cached alongside the road,
all that a juvenile mind
dreamt that his loins were owed
I leave buried behind.

Staff, keep to the path.
I throw away my dear
anger, rising to wrath,
native to me as fear.
Feet, keep to the path.

Class of '72

Imagine living in darkness,
never seeing the sun,
hearing the high Harkness
Tower's carillon
sounding its hourly knells
with fifty-four bronze bells.

Why darkness? I was blind,
lost in a whiskey haze
with Milton on my mind,
stretching exhausted days
with lines of crystal meth,
racing myself to death.

Looking back forty years,
would I change everything,
the *no boy's land* of fears
I wandered? Lord, I bring
such sorrow, such regret
my sins might save me yet.

The Thursday Collection

Thanksgiving was frozen and gray.
Three thousand dollars and change
were donated at our Masses,
and our pastor was moved to arrange
a gift for Dorothy Day,
a thousand three dollar dinners
for the battered, the drunkards, the sinners.
She cares for each person who passes
addicted, alone or astray,
and ours are the souls she would save
as we try to rise out of the grave.

—Sts. Anne and Joachim Church, Fargo

Starting Over

i.m. Alan Sullivan

I draw to the close of my sixtieth year
without you. Still I reach for the phone
every morning, right after I hear
my frail monsignor's baritone:
Through Him, with Him and in Him.

We treasure your versions of the Psalms.
I've starting working for Vincent de Paul's
charity, raising the needed alms
for our parish poor. St. Vincent calls:
Through Him, with Him and in Him.

You perch on my shoulder much of the time,
whether I'm wrong, whether I'm right
on matters of faith, reason or rhyme,
and I trust that we shall reunite:
Through Him, with Him and in Him.

Cathedral of the Prairie

I've come to the Cathedral of the Prairie,
the masterpiece designed by Anton Dohmen,
but first I wander through the cemetery
where many farmers sleep, and like an omen
a dove bursts from a spruce tree. Holy Spirit,
inspire my reading. Wake the dead to hear it.

Behind the graves a field of waving barley
bearded and golden, whispers when the wind blows,
a perfect crop where spirits come to parley,
to watch great-grandsons lay it down in windrows,
Otto and Sigmund, Wilhelm, Helmut, Herman,
yeomen who built this church, most of them German;

yet here's a Timothy and here's a Kevin
and twin spires reaching achingly toward Heaven.

Dream Poem

Dressed in black, he wore a Chassidic hat
but no sidelocks. Not of the Chassidim,
but a Hutterian. I invited him
to cross the threshold of my modest flat.

"What can I do?" "Sir, we seek one to speak
on Schiller, Goethe, Rilke to our boys
and disabuse them of Romantic noise.
We've reason to believe it's you we seek.

We make our boys study the Beowulf.
Our tongue is old. They dimly understand
Anglo-Saxon, and Sir, you've sold us land.
We ask you, Elder, help us cross a gulf

between father and son." "Why me?" I ask.
"Goethe and Rilke I would likely praise."
"We think you know the darkness of these days
and by God's will, you can achieve His task."

This was a dream that verged on the absurd.
Five centuries divide me from these *volk*
who candle chicken eggs for sterile yoke.
Fiasco or disaster? Choose your word.

Yet I admit my grudging admiration
for people who preserve their way, who all
believe God's word was spoken by St. Paul.
They are too few ever to form a nation.

Righteously they gaze up, admire the stars.
They are the colonists God means for Mars.

Address to the Manger

Sleep, infant, sleep
among the oxen and the sheep
which kneel before your manger.
Welcome to danger.

When you become a man
preach us the good news while you can
before you bear the scourge and cross,
an everlasting loss

we all bear to the grave
with guilt. It was your doom to save
us sinners, us ungodly men
whose sins slay you again.

You could have claimed your own
Egypt, a Pharaoh's golden throne.
Instead, Child, you are humbly born
as Gabriel blows his horn.

Ash Wednesday
Joel 2:13-14

In King James Joel asks "Will God repent?"
Modern Bibles tell us the prophet meant
God will "relent" when we are penitent.
I ask a Hebrew scholar for a hint,
crosscheck the Vulgate and the Septuagint.
Metanoia: a change of heart for Lent:
mischievously I ask "Will God repent?"

Wisdom 13:5-9

We worshipped moon and sun,
comets, the circling stars,
Venus and bloodstained Mars,
ignorant of our duty
owed to the unnamed one,
kindler of every beauty
and fire by which we find
the hand, the designing mind
of heaven's artisan.

Triduum

for Frs. Thomas O'Dwyer and Patrick O'Shea
of the Little Flower Church, Hollywood, Florida

I. Washing of Feet

Lawyers and bankers were our honorees
in Fargo, financiers who fund our parish.
But Father Tom crawls on his creaking knees
to honor twelve whose festal garb is garish,
catechumens, half of whom speak no English,
for whom San Marco wrote his text in Spanish.

So Christ washed from his twelve disciples' feet
grit of the shore, grime from the dusty street;
so Mary Magdalene, saved from despair,
dried the feet of our Savior with her hair.

II. Friday Solemnity

I read John's Gospel, fourteen minutes long.
The alto sings Handel's heartrending song,
its words the great prophecy of Isaiah,
the crux and apex of the entire Messiah:
"Despisèd, rejected, a man of sorrow,"
whose wounds heal ours, whose loss restores all loss.
Eight hundred faithful kneel to kiss the cross,
certain that Jesus Christ will rise tomorrow.

III. Easter Vigil

Last night Tom kept one vigil with the dying,
Pat with another, and the softly crying
children and grandchildren watched all night;
the soul so often takes leave at first light.

Térèse, safeguard your aging Irish priests
who preach the Gospel at our highest feasts
but keep their holiest vigils in the dark.
Satan, take aim, and may you miss your mark.

Refusing the Call

Some priests wanted my books signed "Father Murphy,"
figured I'd be their first since "Father Hopkins."
At fifty-eight, I watched how hard they labored,
hospital calls always coming at midnight.
I had a long talk with the Holy Spirit
who speaks Latin: *Domine non sum dignus.*

Four Dispensations

I.
My dear Lord, today is All Souls' Day,
and the Church offers plenary indulgence
to those who attend High Mass, who tend the graves
of their forebears and confess their grievous sins.
A mercy to be claimed or given away,
it is my gift to Michael Donaghy.

II.
My dear Lord, today is All Souls' Day,
and I pray hard for the soul of David Miller
whose son heard my confession just last night.
Today I shall attend my father's grave,
and I'll complete a plenary indulgence
for a farmer who treated me like a son.

III.
My dear Lord, today is All Souls' Day,
and I pray for the soul of my late father
at whose grave I bury the AA medal
which marks nine months of my sobriety.
Let him forgive me all my indiscretions,
and Lord, let him behold your countenance.

IV.
My dear Lord, today is All Souls' Day.
I cradle a box of ashes in my lap,
Alan's. I hope he needs no prayers from me,
but I from him? That is another matter.
His last words to my face were an act of mercy:
"Know when I die, that we are reconciled."

Prayer for Pentecost

I pray for each good priest
who subjugates his will
to yours, who lays your feast
before me. Savior, still
the whirlwinds in their breasts.
Steady them for their tests.
Lord, hear my prayer.

I pray for virtuous men
who never knew your grace.
Each night I plead again,
"Let them behold your face,
love them with your elect."
I pray for Anthony Hecht.
Lord, hear my prayer.

My prayer list for the ill
changes as old friends die,
as my coevals fill
their swelling ranks, and I
whom you have spared so long,
old as I am, stay strong.
Lord hear my prayer.

Lastly I pray for me,
a sinner so long lost,
so blind, I couldn't see
the tongues of Pentecost
descending all ablaze
to teach me thanks and praise.
Lord, hear my prayer.

Our Climbing Days Are Done

Thanks for the gifts You gave:
a partner in my work
to roll up cuff or sleeve
on muscled limbs, and heave
our packs up to a cirque,
for legs that never failed
on any peak we scaled.

My long trail to the grave
leaves ample time to grieve
that which will never be,
the routes we'll never roam
now that You've called him home
and left the wilds to me.

January 25th

Yea, in the shadow of thy wings will I make my refuge
until these calamities be past.
—Psalm 57

Today I'm teaching my first high school class,
Burns Day; and I must brace myself to sing
in a baritone, coarsened by every pass
our Earth makes round the sun, some songs that ring
when snow defends the frozen prairie grass,
when prayers are said for the return of Spring
by those under the shadow of Thy wing.

The Dark Horse

The Muse and I conspired to wreck what beauty
I had at birth. Great bags beneath my eyes
surprise me every morning when I rise.
Offering Her a whiskey seemed my duty.

Granting me poems, pheasants every year,
for decades She led me a merry chase.
She loved my ear, never my freckled face,
my cowboy hat, much less my blue-jeaned rear.

There is a stirruped stallion I must mount.
From his nostrils he whinnies plumes of fire.
How short I fall from passing all desire
besides making the Lord's my last account.

I should repair to Patmos and move on
beyond the Muse who held me so in thrall
when sexual predation was my all,
and study the Long Gospel of St. John.

Third Person

Three Gods in One? It's a perplexity.
I know the Holy Ghost best of the Three.
He is in charge of poets, in charge of one
dove harvester in camouflage with gun.
When I was most bereft, hopelessly lost,
He found me on the Feast of Pentecost,
the very day my friend's blood tests confirmed
how temporary time on earth is termed.

The Sea of Faith

Its melancholy, long withdrawing roar,
my Catholic childhood was a pedal tone
and low vibration of the blood and bone
in the black decades that I tossed at sea.
Like Jonah I was vomited ashore;
now every night a spring tide runs for me.

Delphic Utterance

I have a hole in my heart
scarcely six decades deep,
the cold spring of an art
that floods me when I sleep.

I'd sought a raging river
but sit beside a well.
Seeking a bow and quiver
I found a tortoise shell.

The Holy Time

I. Holy Monday

Were I to dredge the dregs of this machine,
I don't think I'd unearth pornography,
more likely hymns to Christ I've never seen,
clues to the mountainous cartography
a seeker studies on his switchback path
to find God's friendship rather than His wrath.

II. Holy Tuesday

I placed the worst call I have ever made.
You told me Charlotte had become a shade.
You were her spouse, and I her sheltered stray.
Alan shed tears. Four years ago today.

III. Maundy Thursday

Here no priest has the long, luxuriant hair
of Mary Magdalene for washing feet,
but all of us hear Jesus Christ entreat:
        "As do I, so should you,"
and Father Tom unties the unshined shoe
of a young Haitian in St. Vincent's care.

IV. Friday's Altar Boys

It takes three boys to bear it from the porch,
hauling it to the altar of the church
where the believers gathered here today
will kneel to kiss this cross. First I shall say
ninety-two staves, the Long Gospel of John.
Fifteen minutes. Another year is gone.

V. Easter Vigil

A brazier in the aisle—
all of us light our candles,
the alto sings us Handel's
"My Redeemer Liveth,"
and every Christian giveth
a handshake and a smile.

VI. Easter Monday

The Church starts a new year.
Our story has been told,
hoist on a Roman spear,
the bloody robe unrolled,
lots cast at Calvary.

Did we deny Him thrice?
St. Peter's will was free
and God does not throw dice.
Peter and friends were lost
like us. Then Pentecost . . .

and culpability.

VII. Monsieur Vincent's Tuesday

Vincent de Paul. For me, Pierre Fresnay
playing the saint in Nineteen Forty-seven,
his French so perfect I could go to heaven
        quoting him all the way.
Alright, I've packaged pennies in a roll
        to buy a loaf of bread
        when all friends thought me dead
and Caesar's palace was my only goal.
I see a chink of light beside the door
        where Peter greets the poor.

VIII. Thursday, Nine Months After

Love, your successor comes to me at night
or maybe when I nap. He takes your place
only when I am in a state of grace,
which isn't often. Winged, he will alight,
an angel with a head of curly hair
pale as the page at which I sit and stare.

IX. Easter Pastor

It's not the gold leaf on our parish steeple
makes Father Tom so grand a homilist
but love for Jesus and His hungry people.
He clasps the Bible in his massive fist.

I don't like being hugged by bears. You're close
When Father Tom O'Dwyer's arms surround you.
Confession? Whiskey? Both an Irish dose.
If you survive, you figure God has found you.

X. Collins Creek Saturday

Not far north of a village, Parmalee,
I unhitch my bay from a bonneted shay
to cool the mare by a pool on Collins Creek.
The first scarps of the Badlands in my lee,
the Little White River is what I seek
as up the sky the sun has climbed half way.

From the far bank a nervous spike buck stares.
The girl brings me a basket (calico,
gingham, in which of them is she dressed?),
deer sausage, bread, a tin of syruped pears
to feast her cowboy. Waking I think "No,
this never happened a hundred years ago."

Tell me, Father Thomas, for I'm distressed:
how far must a creek carry its snow?

XI. Divine Mercy Sunday

The parish doorbell rings.
When I descend the stair
nobody is there,
only a bag that sings
mournfully by the door,
holding the baby shoes
and little Polo crews
tagged at the Target store.

The Gift

The boy comes to the back door of the parish,
    bearing he says, "A gift."
A crib, its mattress, and a baby bearish
quilt. "I hear you people stand for life."
What came between them, what could cleave a rift
        and birth such sorrow?
        Girlfriend or wife,
she gave her child no chance for a tomorrow
but left a young man sobbing in despair
on the chipped flagstones of my pastor's stair.

Church of Saints Anne and Joachim

for Father Paul Duchschere

Veterans of abortion, heart rending,
like shell-shocked soldiers sending
a message to the world,
three women on a Catholic panel
dream of infants clad in flannel
and the wombs in which they curled.

The Beatification of John Paul the Great

Faustina, greet him on this Holy Day
pledged to your memory and let me say
this little Catholic needs to get to bed.
At Four AM the broadcast starts from Rome.
Six years ago my Pontiff called me home,
knowing that if he didn't I'd be dead.

—May 1, 2011

V. Coda

Two Deaths on the High Plains

The first, September 12, 2003.
The radio said that Johnny Cash was dead.
I was northbound to Canada to see
the ducks and geese throng down, and through my head
and truck speakers his songs came back to me.

The second, April 2, 2005.
The night before I'd dreamed John Paul was dead:
Wilderness Camp, he'd come to me alive
but in the spirit world, and there he said
"*Te Dominus amat.*" A High Plains drive

much like that trek to Canada, no booze,
eight hours, uninterrupted eulogy
save for the weather spots, the sports, the news.
Had John Paul played guitar, I think that he
would have been strumming Folsom Prison Blues.

To You or For You

Father, I visited your grave today,
All Saints, as I have done for many years.
I spoke a sonnet. To allay my fears
you stand beside me as I make my way
through manhood, out of darkness into light.
To you or for you? I pray every night.

High in the Berkshires
for RPW

Richard records in such minute detail
this biosphere, its bounty,
in his synoptic book.
Fern-beds of Hampshire County
recolonize this rarely trodden trail
winding to Hamlen Brook.
Come walk with me, and take a look.
A collapsed, camouflaged pup tent
marks the damp nights youngsters spent
fearing this little wilderness,
grandson and granddaughter
swapping ghost stories, I'd guess.
But suddenly the rush of laughing water
that never deigned to flow
in all my drought year visits long ago:
I stand athwart this mossy, rocky bed,
revolving in my sunrise revery
quatrains I hold in memory
from the best sermon I have ever read.

My Uncle Speaks

Braver than any soldiers that I knew,
mother and daughter slogging on, the two
worshipping God as few of us mortals do.

Tessie was widowed at a tender age,
could have remarried, but she turned a page
to push a chair. How does red hair turn sage?

The mission church? She pushed her crippled daughter,
the roses in her yard? She poured them water,
the turkeys in the shed, she led to slaughter.

I think her pink came from the morning sun,
from upland slopes where white tail spike bucks run
and widowed mothers carry a rifled gun.

Memorial Hospital

"Timmy, Timmy, how did you pull this trick?"
    Drugged out of my brain
    and in substantial pain
    from chomping on my tongue,
    a drunk no longer young,
I looked up at my pastor through the thick
fog of the drug, so lost I was insane,
and heard Tom pray the last rites for the sick.

Paha Sapa Redux

I dreamed of Stonehenge and its megaliths
    rising from mists and myths,
then dreamed of Easter Island and the stone
    giants propped on plinths,
then dreamed of minotaurs and labyrinths.

I dreamed of Rushmore, then of Crazy Horse,
    blasted and bulldozed mountain bone,
and Ziolkowski. Drill the charges, and of course
    stand free of flying stone.

It was Midsummer. The pious at Bear Butte
    tied prayer flags to the trees
  that skirt its breast, its hips, its knees.
So long as pinyon pines bear sundried fruit
    scattered from every cone,
no one, not even Murphy, dreams alone.

Death Thou Shalt Die

for Gail White

Cancer killed a young friend of mine last spring
and killed my dearest friend two years ago.
Now I believe that when the soul takes wing
    to flee our ice and snow,
    the soul is seeking song
and finds redemption where there is no wrong,
where twelve Apostles, all the saints and scholars,
hear English choir boys wearing ruffled collars.

Gratitude

"For you, salvation lies in gratitude,"
said my monsignor on the phone today.
Meditation gave me no quietude,
and though my hair refuses to turn gray
I should be dead, given the course I've run.
I've lived one year longer than did John Donne.

Most of my teeth are clinging to their gums,
Feeney and I still stagger out to play,
I can still scribble rhymes and balance sums
on this, my sixtieth Thanksgiving day,
sunny and forecast to hit forty-three.
Ferchrissakes, Lord, You are too good to me.

Luke XVI and Matthew XXV

for Richard Joseph Christiansen

Sixty measures of wheat?
Eighty measures of oil?
How shall a steward eat,
and how hard must he toil?

Thou gavest me five talents.
Behold! Five talents more.
Christ strikes so fine a balance
fishes beach on the shore.

Master and Commander

One of these nights our Lord is going to say,
"This is my son. I am well pleased with him,"
and you'll not live to see the light of day
    or say goodnight to Tim.

One of these nights our Lord is going to say,
"Charlotte and Richard should be reunited
in spirit, not the resurrected clay
    forbidden the indited

masses who march, backs to the morning star.
It is so near, the gift you think so far."

A Suicide

He blew his brains out not twelve blocks from here,
    a parish rectory.
    The church? Nativity.
Life and not Hell became his gravest fear,
a precipice from which I now steer clear.

Twice I demurred to be ordained a priest,
    but in my grave depression
    I found the intercession
of men who laid before me such a feast
I came to know myself, a famished beast

curled in a den, obsessed with suicide,
    refusing offered hope
    and stumbling down a slope
that leveled only when this chastened bride
of Christ confessed the mortal sin of pride.

Self-murder is the sin you can't confess.
    You're trembling for a drink
    and all around you think
you're a disaster, what have you to bless?
Wretch you may be, our Lord loves you no less.

Mercy

I'm on the flight path of the Life Flight chopper,
and how I hate to hear it whopping over.
An arm jams in a reel of fresh-cut clover,
some boy lies smothered in a combine hopper,
a truck slips from a jack to crush a leg.
"Have mercy on your farmers, Lord," I beg.

One boy lost both arms to a spinning auger,
dialed 911, the pen clenched in his mouth.
The fire department raced from ten miles south,
both arms were iced and reattached. No logger
losing a limb a century ago,
but would have bled out in the North Woods' snow.

When I hear Fargo's Life Flight lifting over,
I know why angels were designed to hover.

Nathan Pitchford

I. Easter Monday

Mon chef majeur? He is the Holy Ghost,
and Nathan asks, "Have you been born again?"
Perhaps not. I have faith in Christ. Amen
I say to you He comes when I am toast
browned on a grill, beside me shredded dove
tossed with the pasta, egg yolks beaten fine
with a wire whisk, a whisper of white wine
and then we garnish with a prayer for love
and Kalamata olives. I am Greek
from way back and invite my friends to dine
however politics or fates incline.
Thrust from the garden, we were made to seek
provender. God told Peter: "Kill and eat."
Temptation: lambs gambol on cloven feet.

II. Journeyman

A year, missionary in Kazakhstan,
a great place for a boy to learn God's plan
    set forth in Ten Commandments
    or Madison's Amendments
to the best rules ever devised for man
    since coal spilled from a hod
    burned for the love of God,
and venison browned in a frying pan.

III. Homecoming

My guest first earned his spurs not far from Pinedale
and spent most of his teenage years on horseback
roaming the wilds, the Wind River Mountains,
his Bible Camp not many miles from Cora,
and followed me up the Green River Valley
to find my fire ring stone cold under Square Top.

I pray the Bible will become his bass note,
the drone string on a gypsy's hurdy-gurdy
above which treble strings ring like the angel's
who harped with David in his ancient city
and now stands guard over a poet's children.
Aged four and eight, let them have saddled ponies.

Heaven on Earth

Here's a deep dream our Lady sent last night:
my cousin's called an idiot savant,
eidetic memory. He cannot write
or read, yet he remembers word for word
each scrap of scripture he has ever heard
at Daily Masses. Satan couldn't daunt
his innocence with Hell's seductive powers,
Christ so much in and with him all his days
that every path he strolls is strewn with flowers.
However absentmindedly he strays,
he's Jeremiah's "sacrifice of praise."

Waking in smiles, refreshed, I know that this
glimpse of serene and inward-gazing bliss
is meant to turn my steps from an abyss.

Spem in alium

Thomas Tallis. I dreamed I typed motet
        but garbled it: motel,
then dreamed I rose on wings of song from hell,
        my flight to heaven set,
soaring above Route 6 in Tonapah.
My teenage ass was wanted by John Law,
but flashing lights aloft were all I saw.

Purgatory

Dignum et justum est: that Murphy stay
in Purgatory until the Judgment Day.
With "Byron lounging grandly at the bar,"
Auden says it's not bad. Nor is it far,
  a few cases of booze away.
Grove of the Poets? I have friends to see
  who knew not God but tutored me,
Mezey and Hecht, expert in prosody,
urging me on when I *gang aft agley.*

There I'll gladly await eternity
before joining the angels in their choir,
    tenors who never tire
but sing for famished souls in need of alms
      King David's Psalms.

On a Verse from Psalm 68

Friend, you were diagnosed at Pentecost.
Reverting to the Church just weeks before,
I read Saint Matthew as my nightly chore,
but you thirsted for David. You were lost,
daunted by onrushing mortality,
so twice I read the Psalms; and then you came
drawn like a June bug to the candle flame
that "shines in a dark place—" eternity.
When told you had only three weeks to live
you buckled down, determined you would save
David your last measure of life and love.

Alan, Monsignor Laliberte came
for lunch: stir-fried andouille and garlic teal.
I gave him two issues of Commonweal,
one with your psalm not "melting before the flame,"
one with my sonnet on the Septuagint,
unrhymed septets, turning on just a hint
of humor, dedicated to your Seree
who gave a year to David, as did you—
a miracle—laboring to make new
the patriarch of lyric poetry,
the Holy Spirit whispering in your ear:
"God, you have looked with favor on the poor . . .
Disperse the nations that delight in war."

Father Tom O'Dwyer

Social justice, respect for property,
love for your neighbor and your liberty—
these are not things easily reconciled.
On poverty and racism, Tom gets riled,
always ready to open wide his door
or raid his wallet for the parish poor.

This is the man gave Alan his last rites
before the ICU turned out the lights.
"The greatest man that I shall ever meet
save Wilbur—" Alan voted with his feet,
beating a path to church, where Father Tom
absolved him with his usual aplomb.

Ursine: Tom is a big bear of a man.
I dreamed he faced a grizzly down. It ran.

Elysium

I dreamed I'd come to view the Elysian Fields
where Greek and Trojan heroes hammer shields
with spears, then laughing, rise up from the fray
to toast each other at the close of day.

A field for battle and a running track,
starters are side by side and back to back.
Pheidippides bears news from Marathon:
"Nenikékamen!" and the war is won.

Parnassus at my back, the scene complete,
the Gulf of Corinth azure at my feet,
rowers set forth to chase the Golden Fleece,
apples are golden and the globe at peace.

Forests and fields lie just north of the Gulf,
teeming with boar and hunted by the wolf.
We rack our spears at sunset. Songs are sung,
and all the hunters and their dogs are young.

Acts 10, 13

In Heaven you'll be twenty-five years old
but know all that you learned in your long lives.
You'll leave the Elysian Fields to bed young wives
once every week. You'll never have to scold
two-year-old dogs. Each bird you shoot, released,
will fly to summon sunrise in the East.
New snow will fall. It will be cool, not cold.

Sam Adams' Ale is running in the creeks,
never a badger nor a rabid skunk
to threaten pups, and when the sun has sunk
and evening's flush is rising in your cheeks,
you'll sit in council at our Father's feet,
sober as angels or a novice monk,
to hear Him say "Rise, Peter, kill and eat."

Parkinson's

i.m. Frederick Ress

I. Tragische Sinfonie

Dum, dum, di dum dum dum,
played by the trumpets and the kettle drum.

Fred once waltzed me carefully through his Mahler.
One, Two and Four were easy, but the late
symphonies stood their guard at Heaven's Gate,
and I, a priestly boy who wore no collar

had much to learn before I could respond
and much to lose, before I could combine
a love of song, fondness for vintage wine,
to mourn a mage laying aside his wand:

our Fred, who took his life rather than face
Parkinson's. I hear *Das Klagende Lied*
from a blond *heldentenor*. His soul is freed
to sing for supper in a better place.

Dum dum, di dum dum dum,
played by the trumpets and the kettle drum.

II. On A Line from Thomas Kerrigan

My friend has Parkinson's. He often falls
and claws his fingernails against the walls,
trying to rise after he's been brought low:
I'm on the run from what? I just don't know.

When Thomas totters, he's the tallest tree
in a dwarf forest. Once every litigee,
motion before him, shivered in the snow.
I'm on the run from what? I just don't know.

Six kids, three wives? Someone take care of him.
He's in the end game, and the end is grim.
I down a shot glass, shake my head, and show
I'm on the run from what? I just don't know.

III. *Ave Atque Vale*

Three times I was in treatment, blocks away,
and Frederick took me in, a chastened stray.
Boddhisatva, really a sort of saint,
Fred spent his decades unsoiled by the taint
of grime that stains such lesser men as I.
His blue eyes were ceilingless as the sky,
but after Parkinson's denied him speech,
he could no longer counsel, no longer teach.
Our tall tenor inhaled his final breath
and leapt twenty-two storeys to his death.

All'alba vincerò. Vincerò!

Marshall Johnson

I wish that I were twenty-six again.
You have a great charge laid on your broad shoulders,
care of the birds that grace our skies. Amen,
Marshall, just look at these erratic boulders
left by the ice. Deep in the wolf cubs' den
we forged our campfires, Paleolithic then.
Gutteral speech, at first just clicks and howls,
snarls when an elder stole away our bones.
Long since I think the hooting of the owls,
their baritones, shivered the eldest stones.
You are a youth, I an old man, both holders
of pedigrees drawn from the dawn of time
when apes beating on logs discovered rhyme.
What must we do? You're way larger than I,
half a foot closer to the cloudless sky,
so big man, stamp your boot on this barbed fence.
Let's go get grouse for which retrievers sigh.
They fly so freely and they pay no rents,
soaring like angels over winter rye.

Three Prayers

I rarely pray to Christ. His sacrifice
was so perfect, it's far beyond my ken.
I'm one of those who have denied Him thrice
but take His bread and wine, then say amen.

I pray three ways, first to the Holy Ghost
in charge of poets who would serve the Lord,
then to St. Michael, head of heaven's host:
"Lead me in battle, angel," I've implored.

Mostly I pray to Mary, for we're told
petitions that she forwards to her Son
are answered always. All of my sins were sold
to Satan, and the sinning isn't done.

Salvation for a creature so defiled?
In my old age I must become her child.

Grateful

What are my gifts? First, three score healthy years.
When Gerard Manley Hopkins was my age
he had been dead twelve years, and not a page
of what I wrote at forty-eight so blears
my eye as Father Hopkins in his prime
however I alliterate or rhyme.
But Hopkins never knew romantic love
which I enjoyed for decades. Every fall
brought our romancing to a dead duck stall
as I pursued the pheasant cock, the dove.
Spring, summer, and winter were for us,
seasons whose memories grow glorious.

Tomàs

I pray each night: Strengthen him for his test,
angels, support him. In his well-earned rest,
        let him behold the face
of Christ, who remembers every worthy trace
of those who sorrow in a state of grace,
but what is grace? In Tom's case, standing tall,
back flat against a red brick Belfast wall,
        singing an ancient tune,
crooning in Gaelic all of *Eileen Aroon*:

Castles are sacked in war,
Chieftains are scattered far.
Truth is a fixèd star,
Eileen Aroon.

Fourth and Forty

You are the kicker tackled at the punt
although little Patrick is wired to go.
So he can track the pheasants on our hunt,
your boy is praying for an early snow.

Maybe he will become an Eagle Scout.
Though Chucky jumps him, often knocks him down,
I have to say I've never seen him pout,
that grin of his, I've never seen him frown.

This is Patrick's first season in the trees,
the cattails and the quarters of wild grass,
licked by a black lab puppy, on his knees,
just six years old. Sunday, and missing Mass.

Apokatastasis

Gail White insists there is a Rainbow Bridge
where all the pets we've cherished lie in wait.
It starts atop a Himalayan ridge,
reaching its terminus at Heaven's gate.
There Boots met Alan when he met his fate.
Waiting for Alan too, were Dee and Maud
to glimpse our Lord whom Satan never awed.

Now Fenian is waiting there for me,
will Puppy be the next? The dead must rise,
so let me run my dogs at Michael's knee
when Hell is harrowed for the Last Assize
and Christ's mercy completes His victory.

One More River

I collect river crossings
often in nightly tossings,
spurring my skittish mare
over each braided ford
   of every stream
      we dare,
and always in my dream
   I meet the Lord
waiting on farther banks
   and tell him thanks.

Father Oliver Herbel

I was expecting a squared hat on your head,
a full beard, not that you couldn't grow one,
a flowing cassock and a stole, blood red.
I am deflated, not that I would know one
Greek Orthodox prelate from the next.
Father, instruct me in some ancient text.

I have a smidgin of Homeric Greek,
not the *Koine* of the latter days
which garbles Hebrew and leaves us to seek
salvation in our Tower of Babel ways.
Pheasant and salmon, I have prepared a feast,
not Corpus Christi, but let me serve as priest.

First I shall listen: the unlikely tale
of a West River cowboy heading east
to St. John Chrysostom, who without fail
leads janissary battles with the Beast.
The Great Schism came in 1054,
but Satan came to Eden long before.

Father, you're young enough to be my son.
You have sworn vows to God and your young wife
I'll never swear, but I can teach you Donne,
sonnets for coaching every man in life,
even a cowboy reared west of the river
where riding east is seeking one's forgiver,

Grandmother's Bible, or the cottonwood
that lords it over an eroded draw
where calves once gamboled, where the windmill stood
and black Conscience perches in trees to caw.
Your blessing, hands on head, before you go.
These lowering clouds smell of encroaching snow.

Po Biz

Alan, the poetry factory grinds on,
24/7, as I dream in verse,
rise to revise four hours before the dawn
and put a modest pittance in my purse.

So far we've published thirty of your Psalms
in the best venues, and your book comes out
next month. Your metrical translation calms
the farmer in me when I dream of drought.

Rejoice, I published three more books last year,
three more in queue, due one year down the road.
When memory falters and I grow unclear
the Holy Ghost applies His holy goad.

For all the smokes and booze, my voice is strong
whether writing, reciting to a crowd,
yet I suspect you won't be waiting long
before I read you David on your cloud.

Awaiting the Birth

Whose soever sins ye remit, they are remitted unto them;
and whose soever sins ye retain, they are retained.
John 20:23

Advent, what does it mean? It means get ready.
Take a tot of rum if you must, to steady
hand and voice before you go to the altar,
leading the ass you are by its greasy halter.

Advent, what does it mean? It means Isaiah,
it means witnessing (you are the pariah),
it means cleansing your soul before the coming
of Jesus, well before the fifes and drumming.

It means searching your conscience, means confession
to one ordained by God, a painful session.
Go turn your heels on every worldly system
and take a long walk through the Book of Wisdom.

Le Rêve

Last night, face to face with myself
    when I was just thirteen,
I told that red-haired, freckled elf
    much of what I have seen.

Clad in a Boy Scout uniform
and a felt Mountie hat,
he couldn't yet forecast a storm,
being too green for that.

I told him "Never take a drink,
    don't smoke, do go to Mass."
Decades transform the ways we think
    as friends and lovers pass

and Labradors become best friends
    when one is growing old.
The eighth step is to make amends
    to all whom you have sold

down the river of your misdeeds,
    the streams of your regret.
Those you'll betray lie in the weeds,
    you just don't know them yet.

The boy's blue eyes grew saucer-sized
    and slightly bleared by tears.
Perhaps he will be less surprised
    than I in fifty years.

Robert Laliberte

I. The Monsignor

Young priests tell me they've climbed into your car
and smelled the scent of roses. Yesterday
my friends gathered at Mass to hear you pray
for a fine poet who has crossed the bar.
The Navy Hymn sent Alan on his way.
You spoke of poetry, the Word made flesh,
how metaphor unravels the dark mesh
of chaos that ensnares us when we stray.

Your learning rouses my Platonic love
and summons this confession: when you preach
or come to grace my table, when you teach
history, Hebrew, Latin, Ancient Greek,
all that your lost host could hope to seek,
I hear the distant wingbeats of a dove.

II. The Confessor

I cook. My dear monsignor comes tonight
for scallop jambalaya, for smoked fish
in a Cobb salad (with his dressing light
to deal with diabetes). None could wish
more penetration of a sinner's mind
than I, so long benighted I was blind.

I call ambition what the priest calls pride,
Superbia, the gravest mortal sin.
This saintly man my Lord took as his bride
looks in your eyes, but deeper, looks within
the Christian conscience where he would anneal
each bloodied soul the Sacred Heart can heal.

III. Partial Indulgence

We always pack my .410 gauge Contender
when Tim and Feeney run game checks in April.
The wilds host nasty varmints who are rabid,
badgers and skunks, dead from a point blank headshot.
So out we tramp, me in my rubber knee boots,
Feeney dressing *au naturel* as always,
checking out pheasants on our favorite pasture.
It's wet as hell and every soaked depression
puts up a pair of hormone-crazy snow geese.
They're all point blank, but I pull out no pistol
until a Canada tries to attack me.
He's immature, I draw and blow him earthward,
then kneel and knife away his bloody breast meat,
sautéed two ways and served with vermicelli,
the cheese, *parmigiano reggiano*.
Red wine reduction, then black bean and garlic.

"Father, I shot a black goose out of season."

"No sin, my son, you're feeding your monsignor."

IV. The Shepherd

Today I fix lunch for a bride of Christ,
student of ancient Hebrew, Latin, Greek.
The eggs and salmon will be finely diced,
and *garni*? It will be onion and chopped leek.

Some forty years since Father was ordained,
and how many confessions has he heard
from the repugnant, from the travel-stained?
How many times has Robert taught the Word?

Tuesdays, Thursdays, I go to hear him preach.
He's only five years older than I am.
I have known masters at majestic speech,
but none of them clasped to his chest a lamb.

V. Apocalypse Tomorrow

"What should I invest in?" asks Father Bob.
"Where does the deeply frightened money flee?"
Licensed to sell securities, I'm asked
this simple question pretty frequently.
From the garage I haul a case of shells,
Winchester, and I lay it at his feet.
"Backpack, canteen. The Bible's in your head.
Boots. When the world ends, you will walk with me,
Feeney will see we have enough to eat.
We'll hike the tracks where railroad cars spill wheat
and pheasants laze until we reach the sea,
and there God will provide for you and me."

VI. The Pilgrimage

Alex Seefeldt

I. Two Pilgrims

The boy and I are going on the road,
our weary shoulders bearing the weighty load
        of David's sacred staves
        as each traveler craves
ale and a fire and some roadside abode.

He set Psalm 27 to a tune
of his devising as he watched a moon
        set on a minor chord.
        Sing a new song to the Lord,
a song no man would wish to end too soon.

Seventeen, he has so much left to learn—
as have I—but Alex awaits his turn.
        No tutor will destroy
        the flicker in this boy,
for he has much fuel in his heart to burn.

II. Archangel

Elfin, he stands so tall
he's not my type at all.
What's with the pointy ears,
eyes welling with tears,
yoked sparrows for his team?
It must have been a dream.

III. *Than longen folk to goon on pilgrimages.*

Another pilgrimage, but where I'll teach
King David, lies three hundred miles away,
so this will be a hard, journeying day.
Lord, curb my tendency to overpreach.

My driver is a blue-eyed, slender youth
who chants verses in four Gregorian tones.
His father tags along. He chaperones
our dates at schools and churches, God's own truth!

The Sullivan Translation: it recovers
metrical music from the Hebrew Psalms.
Each trip we take we give poetic alms
to every soul who braided strands of palms
at Easter, all these people, heaven's lovers.
Over each steeple an archangel hovers.

i.m. Paul Stevens

I've two main types of prayer—
for the sick I ask God to spare
and those for my pagan friends
who meet their untimely ends.
You've moved from one prayer to another,
older brother.

Your life? One of such grace
surely you'll see His face
beyond the Promised Gate.
Let you have long to wait
before a church tower tolls my bell.
Hail and farewell.

Worm Moon

Worm moon tonight, it doesn't spin.
Wish I could say the same of men
and say we do not sin,
spin and foreswear ourselves again.

What holds her smile, her pockmarked face
shining the same when she's above,
is it the ancient trace
of interplanetary love?

The destiny I'll never travel—
I was conceived way too soon
to mine that pile of gravel—
worshipper of the moon.

Friday the Thirteenth

Now the Temple is torn in two
as black clouds veil the sun from view.
A rock is rolled to seal the tomb,
Jerusalem is cloaked in gloom.
A shroud conjures a bearded face,
Christ disappears from our embrace,
and all good Christians kneel to mourn.
Come Sunday we shall be reborn.

E Strings

Surely I mourn the loss of perfect pitch
but learn vibrato only comes with age,
dragging one's sorry self out of a ditch
and dredging meaning from beneath the page.

It's a long drop from the nylon to the brass,
a swoop from boy soprano to the bass
clef where I sing. And looking in the glass,
what has become of my much-freckled face?

I cannot reach three octaves I could range
when only twelve, but I still have red hair,
and every breakfast is the Book of Change,
and every bedtime is a spiral stair.

A Very Private Service

Margaret Thatcher receives the Heavenly Host
in a small chapel beside the parapet
where Michael led his angels and Satan met
ruin. John Paul the Great and the Holy Ghost
concelebrate. The war is not over yet,
but Satan is chipped beef on burning toast.

Why? Because the young are turning away
from lies that inveigled us when we were young.
Over my flowers a gutted hare is strung
to ward off evil. My Shepherd crooks each stray
lamb one at a time. Pray when the sun is slung
westward. Stand watch for the break of day.

Open the Way

Open the Way for God? Take to the road,
Calvary Hill. It is no easy path.
Give up your greed, your tendency to wrath,
go to confession, and lay down your load.

Turn your attention from your sad sack self
to those around you, suffering and in need.
Let no day pass without a kindred deed,
take down the King James Bible from your shelf,

drink deeply, grow like Jeremiah's tree
beside a stream; it flourishes in drought
and casts its shade on all beset by doubt
who follow the hard trail from misery,

hatred of self and others, mortal fright
and suicidal darkness into light.

The Pilgrimage

I. Almost a Franciscan

A long walk up the mountain from Assisi—
My boot heel severed from my right foot Redwing,
I smacked it back, using some broken pavement.
I'd walked my little brother to *l'Eremo,*
some thirty years later I'd be a Catholic.
Now, I suppose I'm almost a Franciscan.

I'd come, not to find God, but the Giottos,
ravishing frescoes for a twenty-something.
The *lingua franca* in the town was Latin,
the only tongue I shared with Filipinas
and three nuns hailing out of far-off China
who watched the sun set on *Rocca Magiore.*

II. *Il Poverello*

Leaving Giotto's frescoed nave,
I climbed from the foothill town
to see the saint's unpainted cave
where Satan was cast down.

The cleft on Mount Subasio
was perilous and wooded,
and the young monk from Gubbio
beautiful but hooded.

He smiled like an angel kissed,
kissed by Giotto's tincture.
Beads were twisted round his wrist;
his waist, bound in a cincture.

He whispered *"Vade retro"*
when the Devil came to parley
and prayed, prayed from *l'Eremo*
for the songbirds and the barley.

III. *Santa Maria degli Angeli*

Jimmy and I hiked to the *Porziuncola*
the day after we climbed a modest mountain
to pay respects to Francis at *l'Eremo.*
The church measures thirteen by twenty-two feet.

The fabled cradle of the Friars Minor,
over it vaults the arch of a cathedral.
A miracle occurred there in the Fifties:
Mary's visage was seen moving and weeping.

A young priest from the North American College,
Virgil O'Neil, among the swooning widows
confessed to a fellow graduate student,
"I just don't see her moving, much less weeping."

A black-clad lady kneeling beside him snapped,
"Father, you have to be in a state of grace!"

Latest Spring Ever
for Dan Miller

I once planted spring wheat on April third,
the year Jack Nicklaus won his fifth green jacket,
his final nine accompanied by a bird,
eagle of course, and the crowds raised a racket.

April eighteenth, will summer never come?
Sheet water, snow drifts in the sheltered trees
recall Boreas, his retreating drum,
as a famished world prays on bended knees.

Farmer, when will you roll into the field
to satisfy for one more year our needs?
When will St. Michael bearing sword and shield
fly to battle with Satan and your weeds?

Roxane

Today I'll meet with an aspiring writer
who grew up near the wide Missouri's waters
in Poplar, Montana, where she was lighter-
skinned than most in town. She has two daughters,
three sons, not what our ranchers call girl thrower.
She's made herself into a first-rate writer
and Master Mistress champion children grower.

Frankly, I think her prose is slightly prolix.
Thursday I go to school to teach King David
to young bulls who will never lose their bollocks
and fourteen-year-old heifers, not yet gravid
with calf, each my Creator's precious creatures.
Longer I live this life, the more I'm avid
to view each of its newly issued features.

Rhina Espaillat

"Extend your life? Just keep teaching the young,"
says Rhina, at the cusp as I grow old.
"Suffer the children to come unto me,"
says Matthew in the middle of his text
about the crucified hung on a tree.
I wake with ninety students to be rolled
reading the Bible, wondering what comes next.

Good Nap

The Holy Spirit calls. My home is open,
my favorite sort-of rhyme for Chaucer's holpen.
Of course I'm sound asleep,
and my Lord Dove has many leagues to go
after he stoops for me in April snow
where dreams run deep.

And what am I to make of nightly visits
from the Lord God, just popping in to kibbitz
at the bedside of a sleeper,
or are these visitations in my dreams
the smoking of a burning barn, its beams,
or something deeper?

Our Lady of the Angels

Irondale, Alabama

I always figured they were fraternal twins,
Fathers Anthony Mary and Mark Mary,
forgiving us for all our venial sins,
and neither one of them is ever chary
of absolution. Forgiveness always wins.

They couldn't have been borne by different mothers,
the one is forceful and the other gentle,
intruding into my messed-up life as brothers.
I watch my Mass, make Lenten soup with lentil
and thank the Lord for my Franciscan others.

Five Couplets

First Kill

I asked the chipmunk, "How fast can you run?"
then blew his brains out with my BB gun.

Flood Crest

A photo shoot framed for the Army Corps
who found my pup and marched him to the door.

Superbia

I begged the Lord when I had grown too tall
"Chop me off at the knees and make me small."

Little Prayer

Holy Spirit, let every day I'm living
occasion a few verses of Thanksgiving.

Buffalo Fence

The Lord says leap. I only ask how high?
It's not far from the High Plains to the sky.

Supplication

Holy Spirit, tonight please come to me.
I need a poem to say on Pentecost,
a great day for the poets who are tossed
like St. Paul or Aeneas out at sea.

Come as a dove, and on my shoulder rest.
Dear Lord, you need not set my hair aflame
as on my birth date, when you breathed my name
to a young redhead, first child at her breast.

Five more would follow as I forged my way,
leaving my adolescence in its wake.
Poetry was the thirst I could not slake.
Pentecost? I need it for Mother's Day.

Sharon's Loss

There is a place where faithful folk abound.
        Imagine it in the air,
        your route, a spiral stair,
it's not a hole dug six feet in the ground.

I pray that there we'll be restored to youth,
        the beauty that we had
        when we were frothing mad,
before our seasoning, our search for truth.

Pentecostal

A dove decides to nest
four feet away from my computer screen,
the window well. It's best
she brood where she'll be heard but seldom seen:

aloft my tallest tree.
That willow shades our little-traveled street
her hatchling doves will flee
as soon as the Lord deems it just and meet.

Red robin wakes at four,
trilling atop a limb that shades my door,
summoning up the sun
which has two hours of darkness left to run.

"Get up! It's Pentecost,"
he sings to hens huddled in modest coats
as nests are drenched and tossed.
A Spirit lends my friends the Gift of Throats.

—May 19, 2013

Rabbit River

Dan Miller called at dawn,
said "Tim, come bring your gun,
they're feasting in the sun
like geese cropping a lawn,
and they're just passing through."

I'd bought a section there
to help Casey and Jon,
Dan's cousins, soldier on
with a square mile of air
which was just passing through.

Danny and I both knew
wherever lay the quest
that summoned us to nest
south of some arctic slough,
we were just passing through.

Manniversary

I trust the Spirit of Truth
when greeting you, restored
you to our risen Lord
and the high spirits of youth.

We'd have marked forty years
last week, except you died;
along with tears I cried
I have shed many fears.

The luck remains so good
my health is holding up.
Today I sail the pup
into a windswept wood;

but back to us, old dear,
each of us at his helm
charting the self-same realm
far from the reach of fear.

Once More the Round

To seek? The less I find,
the harder I must seek
to plumb Augustine's mind.
Though blessed be the meek,

all praise to the bold
who discipline their will,
and Sisyphus who rolled
his boulder up a hill.

Ode for the Mahli Boys

Insufferably Cute

Patrick has reached the fork
of a box elder tree,
Nearer, my God, to Thee.
   He thanks the stork
for bringing a baby brother
   home with his mother.

To Daniel Timothy

When you have wheeled my chair
into the marshes where
mallards and teal descend,
I will be near my end
but still able to shoot,
to sip a little toot
out of my pocket flask
and more, no man can ask.

Platonic Love

Eros denied, *Agapē* was our fate,
given you're young enough to be my son.
I fell for you some twenty years too late
but must admit we've had a glorious run.

We've decoyed mallards where the pintails pass,
hunted morels by boles of aspen trees,
flushed pheasant cocks from the November grass
and shared Communion on our grateful knees.

St. Patrick's Day, 2041

When you open this letter,
I shall be lost at sea,
but I shall be your debtor
for the love you bore to me,
half Irish as I am,
half lion and half lamb.

Danny, I sail the seas
to the Enchanted Isles
with salmon in their leas,
where every boy that smiles
beats on a goat skin drum,
grinning 'til Kingdom come.

Mower's Song

The boy who mows my yard
thinks that he once was I.
He pushes pretty hard
under the prairie sky.
He has no belching motor
or right-hand discharge chute,
no madly whirring rotor,
and he's no longer cute.

Just a front-mounted reel
geared to a rubber wheel,
and that is how the grass
made on the Lord's Third Day
will fall as fragrant hay
until I too shall pass.

Magnum Dove Decoy

for Ellen Mahli

Pope Francis — when a dove
sent from the skies above
perches upon his finger,

all the pilgrims who linger
within St. Peter's square,
fall to their knees in prayer:

"Heaven sends a divine
omen, the Spirit's sign,
for our beloved Pope!"

Dove hunter, I say, "Nope,
the dove decoyed. A white
cassock made him alight,

picture the poor bird's shock!"
"Peter, upon this rock . . ."

V'là l'bon vent

Baby robins, just two days from the egg?
Chucky retrieved them to my blue-jeaned leg,
blue-bodied, yellow beaked, with not a chance
of learning the cock robin's earthworm dance.

A gale had blown. The shredded nest was strewn
across the yard, eviction come too soon.
The hen shrieked in the walnut overhead,
one thumb twist, and the baby birds were dead.

"Nest in the willow, lass," I told the hen,
then said, "Limitless are the hearts of men,"
misquoting Frost, who knew his trees and knew
more than I, his devoted student, do.

The Seven
for Patrick

"Do you believe in angels?" Patrick asks,
unblinking eyes blazing Sirius blue.
I take seriously my senior tasks
and tell my little buddy, "Yes, I do,
Sts. Michael, Raphael, and Gabriel,
an ancient part of me, orthodox Jew;
and I'm convinced Satan was flung to Hell
by archangels and their seraphic host
waging a battle at the walls of Heaven.
Read your Bible, believe the Holy Ghost.
Archangels? I suspect that there are seven,
and I need all the help a man can get.
The angels I dislike I haven't met.

Valhalla

To celebrate the great
first I must praise the small
farmers, the hunters, late
comers to Heaven's gate
or walls at Odin's hall
where we all sit in thrall
purging ourselves of hate,
weregeld and *dom* and fate,
waiting the silver call.

Sixty-Two

Not fit enough to wander the wild woods
or separate my *wouldn'ts* from my *shoulds*
what can I say?

Not spry enough to scamper on a deck
or fend a tall sloop from a leeward wreck,
I steer my way.

No longer lean or lithe enough to climb
a groaning glacier out in Mountain Time,
here I shall stay.

So: on the closely-cropped alfalfa fields
that my Creator in his bounty yields
I stack my hay.

Patrick O'Shea

My soul waits for the Lord
as do we on watch until morning,
more than we who watch for the morning.
—Psalm 130

I.

We charter a large motor yacht
to strew Alan's ashes,
and Patrick says what St. John taught.
The wreath of orchids splashes
into the vessel's foaming wake,
as turbid as my thoughts.
Bow to the wind for Alan's sake,
and motor at three knots.

II.

Mucking the sheep pens in your father's fold,
snatched by Franciscans, just thirteen years old,
Father, what better job than be a priest?
You have learned English, Spanish, and at least
ecclesial Latin. You never fathomed Greek
nor watched a sunset where you didn't seek
some Revelation. You are a chosen one
vigilant at the setting of the sun,
poised at the ramparts as the night draws on,
one of our sentries waiting for the dawn.

III.

Father Tom phones as I am adding leaven
to bread dough, saying Pat has gone to Heaven
to lounge grandly with Alan on his cloud,
leaving his earthbound body to its shroud.

O'Shea and Sullivan, oh what a pair
to draw to, and the drawn cards turn up aces!
I see them limping down my sailboat stair,
nothing but joy and laughter in their faces.

Few priests could rival Pat in *joie de vivre*,
no priest of my acquaintance, a believer
with more fervor. I hope before Pat died
he learned John Twenty-Third, beatified,
was made a saint, for how he loved Pope John.
Now Patrick is a saint, and life goes on
though much diminished, three years to the day
since Alan's death. Remember, we are clay.

Acknowledgements

Poetry published "*Agape*," "Prison Chaplain," "Disenchantment Bay," and the first section of "In David's House." *The Hudson Review* published "The Chase," "Broken Connection, the four sonnets, "Alan's Ashes," and the opening sonnet in "Robert Laliberte." *Light Quarterly* published "Checklist" and "Faith." *Chronicles* published "Mission Church," "Huntress," "*Ecce Canis*," "Soul of the North," "Missing Mass," "Dream Poem," "Hunter's Grace," "Poacher," "II Peter 1:19," and "Adieu." *The New Criterion* published Parts I, III, and IV of "The Second Step." *Gray's Sporting Journal* published "Harvest Moon" and "Posted." *Able Muse* published "Hunting on Thanksgiving," "Prayer for the Virtuous Pagans," and "Winter Wheat." *Sewanee Theological Review* published "To Timothy," "The Axe Head," "One More River," "Beatification," "Sea of Faith," "Third Person," and "Divine Mercy Sunday." *Anglican Theological Review* published "Champion," "To the Corinthians," and the middle three sections of "In David's House." *Commonweal* published "The Thursday Collection." *First Things* published Pt II of "Second Step," "Address to the Manger," "Father Peter," "Nine Bells," "Wisdom," "No Turning Back," "In David's Line," "Father Tom Leads the Faithful in Prayer," and "Wind River Justice." *The Raintown Review* published "Parkinson's," "Life Raft," "To the Chief Musician," "To St. Paul on His Feast Day," "Interment" and the final section of "In David's House." *The Flea* published "The Seven" and "Historian" and "*Jusqu'a la fin du monde*." *SCR* published "The Bowline." *Chimaera* published "*Agnostica*." *The Dark Horse* published "Cross-lashed" and "Remission." "The Last Words of Beowulf" are from the Sullivan/Murphy translation, *Beowulf, A Longman Cultural Edition*. "Sundance" and "Hunting on Thanksgiving" appear in *On Second Thought*, the journal of the North Dakota Humanities Council. *Alabama Literary Review* published "Our 37th Pentecost," "Footsore," "The Parsonage," and "Father's Day." *New Walk* published "Cast a Cold Eye." *Quadrant* published "Survivor," "Class of '72," "Prayer for Pentecost," and "The Mower's Song." *Dappled Things* published "Triduum," "Refusing the Call," "Cathedral of the Prairie," "Third Person," "The Sea of Faith," "Starting Over," and "The Holy Time." *Quadrant* published "High in the Berkshires" and "i.m. Paul Stevens." *Interpreter's House* published "Paha Sapa Redux," "Death Thou Shalt Die," "Yet Another Fall," and "Purgatory." *Able Muse* published "Mercy" and "A Suicide." *Lavender Review* published "Heaven on Earth." *The Dark Horse* published "Elysium." *First Things* published "The Gift" and "Three Prayers." *Anglican Theological Review* published "Father Oliver." *Commonweal* published "Nathan Pitchford." *The Flea* published "Robert Laliberte." *Chronicles* published "i.m. Paul Stevens" and "Worm Moon." *First Things* published "Almost a Franciscan" and "Friday the Thirteenth," "Sixty-Two," and "Open the Way." "*Il Poverello*" originally appeared in *Very Far North*, my third book, and the surrounds of "The Pilgrimage" are prequel and sequel to what I wrote when I was younger. Many of these poems appeared in *Mortal Stakes | Faint Thunder*, published by the Dakota Institute Press in 2011. I apologize to any editors I might have overlooked.

About the Author

Timothy Murphy is a major American poet who lives on the Great Plains. He is a fascinating and complicated man, a child of North Dakota, who writes deceptively simple poetry. He is widely known and admired in Anglophone poetry circles around the world, but not yet widely read at home. Murphy has been a grain and hog farmer, and, like Wallace Stevens, an insurance man, but the twin joys of his life are poetry and hunting. Now he leads the quiet life in a modest cottage in Fargo, North Dakota, where he writes poetry full time, even when he is hunting pheasants with his faithful dog Chucky.

Although his poetry explores such universal themes as faith, family, spirituality, death, farming, friendship, love, and eros, it is all profoundly rooted in place—the Red and Sheyenne River watersheds, in North Dakota, on the Great Plains, at the heart of the continent. Somehow all of it tries to make sense of the windsweep of the northern plains, to explore how place shapes poetry and how poetry shapes one's experience of place. Murphy's poetry, like grain and grass, grows from this place.

Murphy is an unpretentious man with a fabulous poetic pedigree. Robert Penn Warren, his tutor at Yale, passed him on to Richard Wilbur with a note saying, "Because he's the best man we've got." Wilbur's profound faith showed Murphy a way out of his suicidal youth. Acutely aware of man's limitations, Murphy owes more to Thomas Hardy and Robert Frost than to any other predecessors. Like Frost, he doesn't "play tennis without a net."

Born in 1951, Murphy grew up in the Red River Valley of the North. Since he was graduated from Yale College as a Scholar of the House in Poetry in 1972, he has farmed and hunted in the Dakotas. His previous collections of poetry are *The Deed of Gift* (Story Line Press 1998), *Very Far North* (Waywiser Press 2002), and *Mortal Stakes | Faint Thunder* (The Dakota Institute Press 2011). His memoir in verse and prose, *Set the Ploughshare Deep*, was published by Ohio University Press in 2002. With his late partner, Alan Sullivan, he translated the *Beowulf*, which AB Longman published in 2004.

About the Press

North Dakota State University Press (NDSU Press) exists to stimulate and coordinate interdisciplinary regional scholarship. These regions include the Red River Valley, the state of North Dakota, the plains of North America (comprising both the Great Plains of the United States and the prairies of Canada), and comparable regions of other continents. We publish peer reviewed regional scholarship shaped by national and international events and comparative studies.

Neither topic nor discipline limits the scope of NDSU Press publications. We consider manuscripts in any field of learning. We define our scope, however, by a regional focus in accord with the press's mission. Generally, works published by NDSU Press address regional life directly, as the subject of study. Such works contribute to scholarly knowledge of region (that is, discovery of new knowledge) or to public consciousness of region (that is, dissemination of information, or interpretation of regional experience). Where regions abroad are treated, either for comparison or because of ties to those North American regions of primary concern to the press, the linkages are made plain. For nearly three-quarters of a century, NDSU Press has published substantial trade books, but the line of publications is not limited to that genre. We also publish textbooks (at any level), reference books, anthologies, reprints, papers, proceedings, and monographs. The press also considers works of poetry or fiction, provided they are established regional classics or they promise to assume landmark or reference status for the region. We select biographical or autobiographical works carefully for their prospective contribution to regional knowledge and culture. All publications, in whatever genre, are of such quality and substance as to embellish the imprint of NDSU Press.

Our name changed to North Dakota State University Press in January 2016. Prior to that, and since 1950, we published as the North Dakota Institute for Regional Studies Press. We continue to operate under the umbrella of the North Dakota Institute for Regional Studies, located at North Dakota State University.

NDSU NORTH DAKOTA STATE UNIVERSITY PRESS

Index of Titles and First Lines